Proven NOT Guilty

NOT Guilty

Proven NOT Guilty: NOT Guilty

Tommy Rutgersson

Published by Tommy Rutgersson, 2025.

PROVEN NOT GUILTY: NOT GUILTY

First edition. September 5, 2025.

ISBN: 979-8232559748

Written by Tommy Rutgersson.

Table of Contents

Tommy Rutgersson

Printed in the United States of America
First Edition: 2025

Introduction

A not guilty verdict is not silence — it's a decision that the state did not prove what it accused you of.

The judge bangs the gavel. The jurors stand, shuffle papers, walk back to their seats. For a person in that courtroom, the sound is a release and a question at once. *Not guilty* means the prosecution didn't meet the burden of proving guilt *beyond a reasonable doubt*. It is the legal threshold that separates suspicion from punishment, and it exists to protect not just bodies — but lives, livelihoods, and names.

That standard matters because it protects liberty and reputation. In 1992 a group of lawyers and law students launched the Innocence Project to use DNA testing to challenge wrongful convictions and to show what happens when new evidence and better process are brought to bear on old cases (Source: Innocence Project). Their work makes a blunt point: when the system meets better evidence and careful review, outcomes can change dramatically. The message is simple and stark — proof, procedure, and timing matter.

I want to be clear about what this chapter aims to do. This is not a law school lecture. It's not theater. It's a practical, plain guide to help someone standing at the edge of a criminal process make clearer choices. You will find explanation, scene-setting, and tools you can use. By the end, you should feel less at the mercy of the system and more capable of protecting your rights.

The chaos that follows an accusation

When someone hears they are charged, the world narrows. Names on papers look like verdicts. Deadlines appear like traps. I remember sitting in a small conference room with a young man whose voice shook as he described a late-night arrest. He'd been offered a plea on the courthouse steps. The prosecutor talked fast; the public defender was overworked and kind but hurried. He felt pressured to accept something that would get him home sooner, with a promise he could handle the consequences later. Two years on, the plea followed him into job applications and landlord screenings. He had not fully understood his options or the long shadow of a conviction.

This is the core problem: confusion and risk at every stage of a criminal matter. Charges, court rules, and evidence types are complex. People who do not understand their options may accept pleas they do not need to accept, fail to preserve helpful records, or miss crucial deadlines. The result can be lost freedom, job harm, and lasting stigma even when guilt is not proven. The law has technical floors — timelines to request records, rules about preserving physical items, standards for admissible evidence. Miss one step and an avenue that might have cleared a person can close.

But confusion is not fate. Practical, plain guidance makes it easier to protect rights and respond with purpose. That is the promise this book keeps: to turn legal fog into a map.

What this book gives you

Imagine you have a flashlight in a dim house. You can still get lost, but you can also find the exits and the things that matter. This book is that flashlight. It teaches you how to assess a case, gather and preserve evidence, and work with legal counsel to pursue the strongest possible defense. The single practical benefit is concrete: after reading, you will know clear, manageable steps to improve the chances of achieving a not guilty outcome — or, if that is not possible, to resolve a charge with informed choices that protect your future.

You will not find dramatic courtroom fiction here. Instead, you'll find three kinds of help that actually work in the messy world of criminal cases.

First, clear explanations of legal terms and courtroom steps. Words like *arraignment*, *discovery*, *plea agreement*, and *motion to suppress* are not mystical. They are tools. When you know what they mean, you can use them. I will explain these terms plainly and show when each matters, so you make decisions based on facts, not fear.

Second, practical checklists and forms for gathering records, documenting timelines, and preserving evidence. If a police report, video file, phone log, or piece of physical evidence could help your case, you'll have step-by-step instructions on how to ask for it, what to look for, and how to keep it safe. These are the small, often overlooked actions that can shift the arc of a case.

Third, high-level strategy guidance for working with counsel, evaluating plea options, and preparing for hearings or trial. Strategy here is not flair; it's discipline. It's knowing when to press for discovery, when to negotiate, and what to document so your attorney can fight from a position of strength.

A scene: choices at the kitchen table

A few pages in, you might find a man named Miguel (not his real name), sitting at his kitchen table with papers strewn like leaves. He had been charged after an altercation outside a bar. He was tired, angry, and embarrassed. The public defender he met in jail explained a plea that would reduce the charge if he accepted on the spot. Miguel thought the plea seemed fair. It would let him avoid a trial and move on.

We walked through the case by the light of the kitchen lamp. We looked for body-camera footage, witness names, and a record of who called the police. We spoke about his work schedule, immigration concerns, and the long view of a conviction. The plea was still an option, but after securing a few records and consulting a lawyer who could focus on the evidence, he understood alternative paths. That clarity — the knowledge that the choice to plead was indeed a choice — changed the conversation entirely.

That's the practical work of this book: to give you the questions to ask and the records to gather before you sign anything that will shape the rest of your life.

How to think about risk and timing

Timing is ruthless. There are windows in which to demand evidence, file motions, or seek protective orders. There are also softer but no less urgent tasks: contacting witnesses before memories fade, preserving digital evidence that can be deleted, and documenting your own account while it is fresh. The earlier you act, the more options remain.

But action without direction can be harmful. Panic leads to mistakes — speaking to police without counsel, destroying evidence, or rushing into optics that prosecutors can use. That's why this book balances urgency with clear, calm steps: identify the charge, map the deadlines, and secure the first round of records. Those actions create space to evaluate choices and to work with counsel from a place of information, not panic.

What comes next — a practical plan

In the next chapter we start at the beginning. You will learn how to read a charging document so you can tell what you're actually accused of. You will see a simple timeline of the first, most critical deadlines. And you will get a prioritized list — explained in plain language — of the records to secure first: arrest reports, body-worn camera footage, 911 calls, medical records, employment schedules, and any physical items that may be evidence.

Each subsequent section builds toward a practical plan that you can use in real cases. We will move from identification to preservation, then to strategy, and finally to decision — whether that means trial, negotiation, or seeking creative resolutions that protect your future.

A final, practical takeaway

If you remember one thing from this chapter, let it be this: *a not guilty verdict is earned through careful steps, not luck.* The law favors those who know the rules and act within them. Start by getting a clear read on the charge, mark the key deadlines on a calendar, and secure any records that might matter. Reach out for legal help early, and use the checklists in this book to keep the process from overwhelming you.

Turn the next page when you're ready. The first concrete steps — identifying the charge, understanding the timeline, and securing the first records — are simple, but they change everything.

Table of Contents

Chapter 1

Where to find help, how to rebuild, and how to move forward after an acquittal

By the time you finish this chapter, you will know where to look for legal aid and counseling, how to begin restoring your reputation after an acquittal, and what simple, practical steps you can take to put your life back on track. These are not abstract ideas. They are steps people take every day—small moves that add up to steadiness. If you are tired, confused, or still raw from the court experience, that is normal. The good news is you do not have to carry this alone.

Finding legal aid and counseling that fits

When things have been heavy and public, the first question is often: who can help me, and how do I reach them? There are three places people usually start. Nonprofit legal aid groups offer free or low-cost advice for people who qualify. University law clinics let law students, supervised by licensed lawyers, take on cases and give guidance. And public defender offices exist for people who needed a lawyer earlier and may still be able to point you to resources afterward. On the mental health side, community clinics and counselors—sometimes connected to those legal services—help with stress, grief, and the fallout of public scrutiny.

Imagine a small office in a tidy community center. The walls have posters about trauma and rights, and on one wall there's a sticky note that reads, *"You are safe here."* You walk in, a little unsure of what to say. A staff member asks a few gentle questions. That first meeting can be as short as twenty minutes but it's a turning point. You leave with a clearer next step instead of a knot of questions in your chest. That first touchpoint—finding a person who listens and names the next move—matters more than having the perfect plan the first day.

It helps to know what kinds of help are available. Legal aid often follows income guidelines or special status criteria, but many clinics will offer a free initial consultation even if you do not meet every requirement. Schools and community centers sometimes have student-friendly programs with simple intake forms. Counselors tailor their support to your age, situation, and goals. If you are unsure whether you qualify, ask the intake staff: tell them briefly what happened, what you want to achieve, and whether you need help with privacy, records, or emotional support. When someone answers plainly—"We can help with X, Y; here is what you should bring"—the maze becomes a path.

One evening, Lina, a fourteen-year-old, sat in a school counselor's office with her backpack on the floor and the verdict paper folded in her hands. The counselor called a legal clinic the next morning. Two days later Lina attended an intake session where someone explained, in clear language, what documents mattered and what the clinic would and would not do. That kindness—the thought of someone making the call for you—shrinks the mountain. Lina didn't walk into the law alone; the counselor walked beside her.

Start with a short description of your situation, bring whatever official paperwork you have (like the verdict document or court notices), and ask what the first meeting will cover. If transportation or timing is hard, check whether they offer evening hours or virtual appointments. Ask about confidentiality: it's fine to say that privacy is a top concern. Good services will understand and work around those needs. If you find yourself facing confusing or conflicting advice from different groups, pick one primary contact and ask them to help coordinate. That single thread often keeps the rest from tangling.

How to prepare for that first intake

Before the first meeting, gather what you can. A certified copy of the acquittal verdict and any related court documents are useful. These papers are the quiet proof you can show to schools or employers when the time comes. Keep copies in a secure place and note important dates—when you might need to ask for record sealing, for instance. If you cannot get the documents right away, at least have a short, clear summary of what you want: do you want help clearing records, securing privacy, or rebuilding reputation? A one-sentence goal helps intake staff point you in the right direction.

When you call or email, a short script works. You might say: *"Hello, I'm seeking guidance after a not guilty verdict. I'd like to understand what legal aid options and counseling are available, and what I should bring to an intake."* That sentence opens a door. If you prefer email, a brief subject like "Request for legal aid and counseling after acquittal" helps staff prioritize your message.

Kai, sixteen, wanted to protect his privacy. He called a youth advocacy hotline and was surprised at how calm the staff was—no judgment, just practical steps. They walked him through how to prepare for appointments and what questions to ask about record sealing. Having someone outline the path kept him from spinning into worry.

Coordinating legal and emotional support

Legal advice and counseling complement each other. A lawyer explains what the law allows; a counselor helps you manage feelings and relationships while you take those legal steps. If you have a school counselor, a trusted teacher, or a mentor, invite them into the conversation at the level you feel safe with. Keep a simple contact list of the people helping you and share updates you are comfortable sharing. That list need not be more than a page in your notebook—names, roles, and the best way to reach them. When your supports know the plan, you can act with more confidence.

If you need help finding services, look at community mental health centers, university legal clinics, or national organizations that offer helplines for youth. Often these services are linked, and they can point each other toward the right person for your situation.

Restoring your reputation: a step-by-step approach

An acquittal does not erase what happened in people's minds. Rumors, misunderstandings, and worry can linger. Rebuilding reputation is a slow work of steady choices. It starts with paperwork and moves into everyday behavior.

First, secure your official records. Ask for a certified copy of the acquittal and any other court documents that show the outcome. These records are important when you need to speak to a school, employer, or landlord. Keep copies in a safe place and consider making digital scans stored in a password-protected folder.

Next, learn about record-clearing in your jurisdiction. Some places allow charges to be sealed or expunged even after an acquittal; others have wait times or specific conditions. A legal aid attorney or clinic can explain what's possible where you live and what steps to take. Understanding the rules prevents you from accidentally sharing information before it's safe to do so.

When you need to talk to schools or employers, prepare a short, calm explanation. Stick to the facts you are comfortable sharing and avoid over-explaining. For instance, you might say, *"I was acquitted of the charges, and I am focused on moving forward. Here are the court documents to show my status."* Ask a trusted counselor to help you write a brief note for administrators if that feels easier. A clear, factual statement often deflates gossip faster than silence or defensiveness.

Ari, fifteen, feared the verdict would ruin his college chances. He asked his guidance counselor for help and together they gathered a sealed-record letter from the court and a short, truthful statement for application reviewers. Ari also began volunteering, not to prove anything, but because caring for others helped him feel like himself again. Over time, the steady proof of consistent character carried more weight than any explanation.

Rebuilding trust also happens in the small, daily ways. Attend classes, show up at work, meet deadlines, and be consistent in your actions. If possible, ask for references from teachers or supervisors who can vouch for your behavior. When your application or a future employer sees a record of reliability, it quiets rumors more effectively than argument.

Maya, seventeen, chose to speak directly to her part-time supervisor. She brought a copy of the acquittal documents, explained briefly that she had been acquitted, and said she wanted to focus on dependable attendance and steady work. Her supervisor appreciated the honesty and the plan. Within weeks, Maya's regular presence and consistent performance rebuilt trust.

Practical steps you can take right now

There are simple, concrete moves that make a big difference. First, list three nearby legal aid options and counseling services and write down how to contact them. Second, collect your case documents—verdict paper, court notices, and any correspondence—and store them in a folder. Third, write a short, honest statement of your goal: do you need record-clearing, help with school conversations, or emotional support? Fourth, pick one person to call first and set an appointment within the next week if possible. These small tasks are not dramatic, but they build forward motion.

If you do not hear back from an organization, follow up with a polite call or email. Sometimes delays happen; a gentle reminder will move things along. If someone gives conflicting advice, return to your primary contact and ask them to help coordinate or suggest a reliable second opinion.

Moving forward after a not guilty verdict: rebuilding your daily life

A not guilty verdict can bring relief and confusion at once. Even without legal guilt, stigma can feel heavy. Protecting your mental health is not optional; it is the foundation for everything else you will do.

Create a routine that supports your wellbeing. Simple things like regular sleep, balanced meals, a short walk, and time with friends or family create a base of steadiness. If feelings of shame, anger, or anxiety persist—or if you struggle to sleep or focus—reach out to a counselor. Peer support groups can be especially helpful: talking with people who have gone through something similar reduces loneliness and gives practical tips.

Set small, achievable goals for school or work. Maybe it is attending three study sessions each week or volunteering a few hours. Small successes rebuild confidence. Re-engaging with clubs, teams, or community service gives you places to be judged for what you do now, not what happened before. These connections produce mentors—coaches, teachers, or supervisors—who can offer practical advice and letters of support when needed.

Omar, sixteen, felt invisible at school after his case. He started tutoring younger students at the community center and joined a service club. Teaching others reminded him of his strengths and gave teachers fresh reasons to see him in a new light. Within weeks, invitations to study groups followed. The change came from steady action, not fireworks.

If you are thinking about a civil claim because you believe you experienced harm during the legal process, speak with a trusted advisor before moving forward. Civil actions can be appropriate, but they are complex and emotionally draining. Gather evidence, ask questions about timelines and costs, and get a clear sense of realistic outcomes. A careful, deliberate approach prevents more stress and keeps you in control of your decisions.

Troubleshooting common problems and how to handle them

Things often do not go in a straight line. You might feel overwhelmed by conflicting advice, worry about privacy, or make a quick statement you later regret. These are fixable.

If you get mixed messages, call your primary contact and ask them to help coordinate. Say, *"I'm getting different advice—can you help me sort this out?"* If privacy is your concern, ask directly about confidentiality policies and what information may be shared. Keep records of who you speak with and what was discussed—date, time, and a sentence summary. That simple habit prevents confusion later.

If you feel tempted to speak or act before you understand record-clearing rules, pause and ask for clear written guidance from a legal advisor. Rushing often creates new problems. If you don't hear back from a resource, follow up once with a polite note. If delays persist, ask whether they have walk-in hours or an alternative contact.

Words that help: scripts you can use

A short script saves energy and reduces the chance of oversharing. For intake calls, you can say: *"Hello, I am seeking guidance after a not guilty verdict. I'd like to understand what legal and counseling options are available, what I should bring, and how soon I can meet with someone."* For an email to an organization, try: *"Subject: Request for legal aid and counseling after acquittal. Dear [Organization], I recently received an acquittal and would like to learn about free or low-cost legal advice and emotional support. Please let me know what documents I should prepare and how soon I can meet with a counselor or attorney."* These short messages create clarity and show you are ready to act.

A closing note and the next step

Restoring life after an acquittal takes practical steps and quiet courage. Gather your paperwork, reach out for legal and emotional help, and choose one action this week—a call, an appointment, a short email. Those first moves are the scaffolding for steadiness.

You are not defined by the worst days you have lived through. Over time, people will judge you by the pattern you build: steady attendance, honest communication, and consistent, positive behavior. That pattern is more persuasive than any argument.

The next chapter will look at how the legal system treats not guilty outcomes in more detail: what rights you retain, what protections may exist for your record, and how to work with lawyers to secure the outcomes you need. For now, be kind to yourself. Take one small step, make one call, and keep a record of who helps you. Those quiet acts move you forward.

Thank you for making the choice to read this chapter and for taking steps toward rebuilding. You're not the first person to start here, and you won't be alone as you go on.

Chapter 2

The Legal Process Leading to a Not Guilty Decision

The courtroom had the tired light of late afternoon. Outside, a drizzle embroidered the windowpanes; inside, the air smelled faintly of old paper and coffee. A man sat at the defense table with his hands folded, and across the room a young prosecutor rifled through a file as if the pieces of paper could be assembled into a whole. The jurors watched with a kind of polite hunger—faces that tried to be neutral but could not hide a personal stake in every pause, every unsteady glance.

That quiet room is where outcomes that change lives are decided. The path to a not guilty verdict is not a single event. It is a sequence of stages, a tug-of-war of narratives, and a delicate balancing of rules about what counts as truth. To understand how a jury returns a not guilty verdict, you have to walk through the legal choreography: the labels of offense and defense, the moments where evidence is admitted or rejected, and the way persuasive stories are constructed and dismantled.

From Arrest to Arraignment: The First Movements

The legal dance often begins long before a courtroom drama is televised. An arrest can follow a 911 call, a traffic stop, or a police investigation. That initial moment—hands on cuffs, lights flashing—changes a life, but it does not yet determine guilt or innocence. The next formal step is usually charging: prosecutors review the police investigation and decide whether to file charges. Some cases never move beyond this stage because the prosecutor sees holes in the evidence or believes the chances of conviction are too low.

When charges are filed, the defendant is brought to an arraignment, a short hearing where the accused hears the charges and enters a plea. It is a procedural moment, but meaningful. The plea—guilty, not guilty, or sometimes no contest—sets the immediate course. Plea bargains are often offered at this stage and throughout the pretrial period. For many cases, a plea deal ends the process; for others, the defendant insists on trial. Insisting on trial is a gamble. It can mean months of maneuvering, but for those who truly believe they are innocent, it is sometimes the only acceptable path.

Throughout these early stages, the prosecution and defense begin showing their hands. The prosecutor decides which charges to press and how aggressively to pursue them. The defense counsels examine the state's case for weaknesses—flimsy witness statements, tainted evidence, or constitutional mistakes in how police gathered proof. Early motions may ask a judge to suppress evidence allegedly obtained after an unlawful search, or to dismiss charges for lack of probable cause. These disputes are the first time judges weigh what evidence a jury will ever see.

Discovery and Pretrial Battles: Feeling Out the Case

Discovery is where the contest becomes methodical. The prosecution must turn over evidence it plans to use. Police reports, witness statements, photographs, lab results—these items are laid bare for the defense to inspect. In return, the defense may also disclose certain materials, though rules differ by jurisdiction. Good discovery is less cinematic than it sounds; it is a pile of files, a parade of emails, and sometimes, a missing bit of paper that becomes crucial.

Pretrial hearings can be like skirmishes before a battle. Defense lawyers file motions to exclude evidence—challenging lab results as unreliable, or contending that a witness's statement is hearsay. Prosecutors counter with legal theories meant to keep the jury from seeing the defense's strongest reasons for doubt. Judges decide what the jury will be allowed to hear. A motion to suppress, if successful, can fragment the prosecution's story. If that story collapses without a vital piece of evidence, a not guilty verdict becomes more likely.

Here the roles are clear. The prosecution builds a legal argument that the accused committed the crime beyond a reasonable doubt. It must set up facts and present admissible evidence. The defense's job is not to prove innocence; it is to show the jury that the prosecution's case fails to meet its burden. Sometimes that is done by producing alternative explanations. Sometimes it is done simply by undercutting the prosecution's evidence until doubt seeps through.

Jury Selection: Choosing the Lenses of Judgment

Trial-level decisions are filtered through human minds. Jury selection—voir dire—is the process of selecting those minds. Prospective jurors answer questions about their backgrounds and beliefs. Attorneys for both sides seek jurors who may be favorable to their story or impartial enough to weigh the case fairly.

In this quiet interchange, lawyers read faces and listen for subtext. A defense attorney might push to exclude someone who says they distrust people who "play fast and loose" with the law. A prosecutor might hesitate to challenge a juror who shows sympathy for victims. The chosen twelve—along with alternates—will be the tribunal that listens, analyzes, and ultimately decides. Jury instructions, given at the close of trial, will tell them the legal standard: the prosecution must prove the defendant's guilt beyond a reasonable doubt.

Opening Statements: The First Stories

Once the jury is seated, the trial begins. Opening statements are the first deliberate storytelling: promises about what the evidence will show. The prosecutor lays out a narrative: time, place, motive, act. The defense offers a counter-narrative—sometimes a direct denial, sometimes a promise to show that the prosecution's story is incomplete.

These statements are not evidence, but they set frames. Good openings are economical and vivid. They sketch a timeline, name key witnesses, and plant the central theme: trust this evidence, or consider the holes. A juror leaves the room not with certainty, but with a mental map of the battle ahead.

Witnesses, Testimony, and Cross-Examination: The Heart of the Case

Witness testimony is where evidence becomes human. Eyewitnesses describe what they saw. Victims describe what happened to them. Police officers explain how they investigated. Experts translate DNA results, ballistics reports, or the patterns in financial records. Each witness brings a voice to the story, and each voice can be strengthened or weakened under cross-examination.

Cross-examination is the defense's sharp tool. It is where inconsistencies are highlighted, where memory lapses become reasonable doubt, where motives for error—fear, bias, poor lighting—are revealed. Prosecutors will do their own cross-examinations, sometimes aiming to neutralize defense witnesses or to shore up their own evidence.

Evidence comes in many forms. Direct evidence—an eyewitness who saw the act—can be powerful but also fragile. Memory is a poor recording device; it skews with stress, distance, and suggestion. Circumstantial evidence—patterns and inferences—can be persuasive when it coheres into a story, but it rarely speaks with the same apparent immediacy as direct testimony. Physical evidence, like fingerprints or DNA, carries an aura of certainty but is only as strong as the chain of custody and the laboratory processes behind it. Even forensic science, once seen as infallible, has limits and error rates. One broken link—an undocumented transfer, a contaminated sample—can turn what seems like ironclad evidence into an opening for doubt.

A moment I often think about came from a small county trial I watched years ago. A single white glove was introduced as physical evidence connecting a defendant to a burglary. It seemed straightforward until the defense called a clerk from the evidence room. She testified about the drawer in which the glove had been stored—an overstuffed drawer where items were sometimes placed without clear labels during long shifts. Suddenly the glove was not an unbroken chain to the scene but a cloth item that had been handled by many hands. The prosecutor withdrew the glove from contention. What had seemed like a slam-dunk became a hinge on which the jury might swing away from conviction.

Objections and Rules of Evidence: Who Decides What Counts

Trials are not just about facts; they are governed by rules. Lawyers stand to object when testimony violates rules of relevance, hearsay, or privilege. Judges make rapid calls to admit or exclude. Those decisions shape the jury's view.

A judge might exclude a statement made to the police because it was not given after the defendant was properly warned of their rights. The exclusionary rule exists to prevent evidence obtained in violation of constitutional rights from being used at trial. It is controversial, but it can be decisive. When crucial statements are suppressed, a prosecutor's case can be rendered materially weaker.

Closing Arguments and Jury Instructions: The Final Pitches

After the evidence is closed, lawyers make their final iterations of the story in closing arguments. The prosecutor will argue why the totality of evidence meets the legal standard. The defense will insist that uncertainties remain—facts that do not fit, explanations that the prosecution never addressed.

Then the judge instructs the jury on the law: what elements the prosecution must prove, how to think about eyewitness testimony, how to handle reasonable doubt. These instructions are legally precise but rarely gripping. Still, they are the mechanics that convert doubt into acquittal. Jurors are told that if they have reasonable doubt about any essential element of the charge, they must return a not guilty verdict. That legal standard is the hinge where the abstract idea of "reasonable doubt" is translated into a decision that can free a person.

Deliberation: The Quiet Work of Decision

Jury deliberation is private. Images of strained faces, heated arguments, and the slow tally of votes are often dramatized. In reality, deliberation is a mixture of careful sifting and emotional negotiation. Jurors compare memories of testimony, revisit the weight of particular witnesses, and sometimes replay a single line of cross-examination that unraveled the prosecution's case.

Deliberation shows how evidence functions not only as a set of facts but as a story woven by people. A strong narrative can make circumstantial pieces cohere; a weak narrative leaves pieces that do not fit and invite alternative explanations. Jurors bring their own experiences—some relevant, some dangerously idiosyncratic. The foreperson's role is to keep discussion moving and to seek a consensus in the face of reasonable disparities.

The Verdict: Not Guilty and What It Means

A not guilty verdict is not a factual declaration that the defendant did not commit the act. Rather, it is a legal judgment that the prosecution failed to prove guilt beyond a reasonable doubt. It is a threshold decision, a public declaration that the state has not met its burden.

For the defendant, not guilty means legal freedom from that charge. It also means the judge cannot later try the same person for the same offense—double jeopardy prevents re-prosecution on the same facts. For victims and communities, a not guilty verdict can be wrenching. Many people leave the courtroom with unresolved emotions: relief, anger, confusion, or a sense of injustice. The system prioritizes a high standard of proof precisely because the consequences of convicting an innocent person are considered profoundly worse than acquitting someone who may, in human terms, be guilty.

How Evidence Influences the Verdict: Weight, Credibility, and the Burden of Proof

At the center of a not guilty finding is evidence and how jurors interpret it. Evidence influences verdicts in three main ways: admissibility, weight, and credibility.

Admissibility is the gatekeeping function. If a judge rules evidence inadmissible, the jury never sees it. This is a powerful decision. A suppressed confession or a tainted forensic report can strip the prosecution of its most compelling arguments. The defense often seeks to exclude evidence precisely because its presence would allow the prosecutor to construct a compelling story.

Weight refers to how much force a piece of evidence carries once admitted. DNA evidence often looks heavy on the scales because it points to statistical probabilities. But even DNA requires context: whose DNA was it? Where was it found? Could transfer account for its presence? Photographs are persuasive, but they can be ambiguous; a photo shows a slice of time, not the why or how.

Credibility is the human judgment about whether a witness is telling the truth or whether an expert is interpreting data honestly and competently. Cross-examination is designed to test credibility. Jurors are asked, in effect, whether they trust the witness's memory, perception, and motive. A shaky witness can make even strong physical evidence seem less decisive if jurors begin to doubt chain of custody or handling procedures.

The burden of proof is the rule that determines the outcome. The prosecution must remove reasonable doubt. Reasonable doubt is not an abstract obstacle; it is a standard rooted in common sense. If a juror, after seeing the evidence, hesitates about any element of the offense for a reason that is logical and not speculative, they are required to acquit. That standard is the safety mechanism that protects against convictions based on shaky evidence.

The Power of Narrative: How Stories Win or Lose Cases

Beyond rules and forensics, human beings decide cases. People understand the world through stories. A coherent prosecution narrative that aligns witnesses, timelines, and physical evidence can be compelling. Conversely, if the defense can poke holes in the narrative—showing inconsistencies, alternative explanations, or bias—the story can unravel.

Trials are often contests of coherence. Which story makes the most sense? Which version of events explains the most pieces without needing improbable assumptions? Jurors are natural storytellers; they will fit facts into a story even if it requires ignoring uncomfortable details. Attorneys work to make sure their story is the one jurors accept.

When Not Guilty Feels Unfinished: The Human Aftermath

A not guilty verdict ends a legal process, but not wounds or reputations. People who are acquitted may still face social stigma, job loss, or community suspicion. Conversely, those who believed a crime occurred may feel the system failed them. The law clears the record legally, but it does not always restore the emotional balance.

For legal actors, a not guilty verdict is sometimes a validation of process—the safeguard functioning as intended—and sometimes a call to improve investigations, evidence handling, or support for victims. For the public, a single verdict can be read in many ways: as a triumph of constitutional protections or as a failure to obtain justice.

Takeaways: How the System Protects Against Error and What Still Matters

If you leave the courtroom one lesson clearer than the rest, it might be this: evidence matters, and its admission, interpretation, and presentation determine outcomes. The law sets a high bar for conviction because it values protecting the innocent. Yet the system depends on humans—officers, scientists, lawyers, jurors—each prone to error, bias, or fatigue.

For anyone watching or involved in a criminal case, a few practical truths help make sense of the process. Understand that early hearings shape what a jury sees. Know that the prosecution bears the burden of proof. Appreciate that not every convincing story is supported by admissible evidence. And recognize that cross-examination, motions, and jury instructions are not mere formalities; they are the mechanisms that convert factual disputes into legal outcomes.

A Quiet Ending

When the court went silent and the jury filed back into the room that rainy afternoon, the jurors' faces were unreadable. The foreperson cleared their throat and spoke the words that altered lives: "We find the defendant not guilty." There was a small exhalation in the defense table, a visible slump in the prosecutor's shoulders, and then the soft sound of shoes on linoleum as people began to stand and move. Not guilty. Two words that signal the conclusion of a legal story, and the beginning of everything that follows.

In the end, a not guilty decision is not a simple vindication. It is the outcome of a process designed to protect liberty by demanding rigorous proof. It asks us to live with uncertainty—sometimes painful, sometimes necessary—and to respect the rules that make justice possible even when the results are not entirely satisfying. The law's insistence on proof beyond a reasonable doubt is a stern friend: it is unforgiving when the evidence is thin and relentless when it is strong. That tension is not a flaw but the system's heart.

Chapter 3

A jury says "not guilty." The room exhales.

The words are simple, two syllables that fall heavier than anyone expects. They hang in the air like steam from a mug on a winter morning—visible, then gone—but their heat lingers. If you have ever sat in the back of a courtroom, watched a set of strangers bury their heads to read a verdict, and then listened as the foreperson speaks those words, you know the moment comes with a rush of many things: relief, anger, confusion, and a kind of stunned quiet. For some, *not guilty* feels like vindication. For others, it is a painful, baffling denial of wrong.

People often hear the phrase and think it means the defendant is innocent. Sometimes it does. Sometimes it does not. The law and the human stories inside that law are messier than the headline. Behind every not guilty verdict are reasons—legal, evidentiary, and human—that can be as mundane as a missing lab report or as weighty as a constitutional right. This chapter explores three of the most common reasons juries return a verdict of not guilty: insufficient evidence to meet the burden of proof, successful legal defenses and procedural errors that force dismissal of evidence, and the simple, stubborn fact that witnesses and evidence can fail to persuade.

I remember one winter afternoon, years ago, sitting in a courtroom with my coat still damp from the snow. The defendant was a young man with tired eyes. The prosecution had presented a string of witnesses—neighbors, a few police officers, a forensic analyst who spoke in careful, academic tones. The defense wore a patient, waiting silence. When the jury came back, the foreperson stood, read *not guilty*, and a woman in the gallery began to sob. She later told me she had been certain of what had happened. She had been certain the system would choose right. That day I watched how fragile certainty can be when it faces the legal standard built into our system: beyond a reasonable doubt.

Insufficient evidence: the burden that shapes every verdict

Our legal system makes a deliberate choice: it is better that ten guilty people go free than one innocent person be convicted. That famous aphorism captures a moral and legal judgment, and it is why criminal cases rest on a burden of proof called *beyond a reasonable doubt.* The phrase sounds grand, but in practice it raises a simple, very practical bar. Evidence must not just suggest a defendant might be guilty. It must convince a reasonable person, based on the evidence presented, that the only sensible conclusion is guilt.

What does that feel like in a courtroom? Imagine the state builds a case on a partial fingerprint on a glass, a witness who saw someone "similar" to the defendant, and a cell phone ping near the scene. Each of those facts alone might point toward guilt. Together, they can be persuasive. But if the fingerprint is partial and lab reports say it could match several people, the witness's memory is shaky, and the phone ping only places a device within a broad area, those same facts can leave gaps. In the quiet of jury deliberations, those gaps become reasonable doubt.

A small scene can make this clear. Picture a jar on a shelf. The jar is full of marbles; some are blue, some green. If you reach in without looking and pull out a blue marble, you might guess the jar holds mostly blue marbles, but you cannot be sure. The pieces of evidence in a trial are like those marbles. One blue marble will not tell you the jar is full of blue marbles. Prosecutors must show enough blue marbles—coherent, consistent, well-documented pieces—that the jar's color becomes evident. If those marbles are missing, broken, or ambiguous, a juror can reasonably refuse to fill in the gaps.

Insufficient evidence plays out in many concrete ways. Sometimes forensic tests are inconclusive. DNA might be degraded, or an analyst may report that the profile is partial and cannot uniquely identify a person. Other times, surveillance footage may be grainy, leaving the identity of the person in the frame uncertain. Phone records can show a device's general movement but not who held it. A witness might have seen a troubling event from across the street, in poor light, and their memory may change when asked the same question weeks later. Each of these shortcomings chips away at a case.

Juries are human. They bring instincts and life experience into deliberations. Many jurors are understandably reluctant to convict on shaky evidence. They have to be convinced not by certainty in an absolute sense—since perfect knowledge is rare—but by practical certainty. When evidence leaves space for *another reasonable explanation*, the law favors acquittal.

Successful legal defenses and procedural errors: when the rules protect rights

The law is not only about proving facts. It is also about the way the state must obtain those facts. There are rules—some long-established, some developed in courtrooms through decades of fights—that protect people from overreaching investigations and ensure fairness. When those rules are broken, the court can exclude evidence or even dismiss a case.

Think of procedural rules as the guardrails on a mountain road. They keep investigations within a path that protects constitutional rights. If authorities veer off the road—by conducting an illegal search, for example—the evidence collected during that deviation might be tossed out. Without that evidence, what remains can be too weak to convict.

One common procedural issue is an illegal search. The Fourth Amendment in the United States protects people against unreasonable searches and seizures. If police search a home without a warrant and without an applicable exception, the items they find may be excluded from trial. The effect can be dramatic. I once sat near a defense attorney who, with quiet intensity, argued that a search had been illegal. The judge listened, sifted through the testimony, and agreed. The key pieces of physical evidence disappeared from the case. What seemed like an open-and-shut matter suddenly lost its center.

Another procedural pitfall is the treatment of confessions. Police use many tools to gather information. But when the confession is the product of coercion, deception, or a failure to provide a known right—like the right to remain silent—the court may rule it inadmissible. Miranda warnings and the protections they afford are not mere formalities; they address the human tendency to say what is needed to stop pressure or pain. A judge's decision to exclude a confession can change the balance of a trial.

Then there are successful legal defenses that do not rely on technicalities. Self-defense is a classic example. If a person reasonably believes they are about to be harmed and uses force to stop the harm, they can be justified in what they did. The same act can be criminal in one context and lawful in another. Similarly, a defendant might present an alibi that places them elsewhere during the time of the crime. If the alibi is corroborated by credible witnesses or surveillance footage, it can undercut the prosecution's timeline.

Procedural errors can also arise from the way investigators manage evidence. Chain-of-custody issues—when it's unclear who handled a piece of evidence and when—can make a juror wonder if evidence was contaminated or altered. Lab reports that lack documentation or that come from labs with poor practices can be attacked. Prosecutorial misconduct—such as withholding exculpatory evidence or making improper statements to the jury—can also lead to acquittal or a judge's instruction that taints a case beyond repair.

The ordinary human reactions to stress complicate this. Police officers and prosecutors work under pressure. Mistakes happen. But the legal system prioritizes rights in part because mistakes, when they occur, can lead to wrongful convictions. The rules about evidence and procedure may frustrate a victim or a community seeking closure. They may feel like loopholes. But those rules serve a restraint purpose: they hold the state to a standard because the consequences for individuals are so great.

Credibility: when people and evidence simply don't persuade

At its heart, a trial is a battle of stories. Each side tells a story: what happened, who was involved, why it matters. Jurors decide which story to accept. Often, the deciding factor is *credibility*—who seems believable. Credibility is fragile. It depends on memory, honesty, consistency, demeanor, motive, and technical reliability.

Eyewitness testimony is one of the most powerful yet fragile forms of evidence. People believe what another person claims to have seen. But human memory is not a videotape. It is malleable. A witness can be sincere and still be wrong.

Lighting, distance, stress, time, and even the way questions are asked can all alter recall. Cross-examination can undo an eyewitness's certainty by pointing out gaps or inconsistencies that creak under pressure.

Consider the small human detail of how we speak when we are nervous. In the courtroom, a witness who speaks haltingly, contradicts earlier statements, or becomes evasive under simple questioning loses weight. Jurors pick up on tone and eye contact in ways that are both intuitive and sometimes unfair. A person with autism or social anxiety might appear less credible despite telling the truth. Conversely, a confident, polished witness can seem more believable even when their testimony has problems. Defense attorneys know this and often train witnesses to highlight inconsistencies and biases.

Expert witnesses, too, can be sources of doubt. Forensic science carries a veneer of certainty—DNA, ballistics, toxicology. But not all forensic fields are equally reliable. The way an expert phrases a conclusion matters. If an analyst suggests a likelihood but then overstates certainty in the courtroom, cross-examination can expose the gap. Jurors then face a technical contested field and may choose the safe path: doubt.

Bias is another layer. Witnesses can have reasons to shade the truth. A witness close to the defendant might minimize wrongdoing; a witness with a grudge might magnify it. Informants who trade cooperation for leniency have obvious incentives. Jurors are taught to consider motives, but sometimes the influence of an incentive is subtle and only becomes obvious when probed.

The credibility of physical evidence can also be undermined. A lab sample that sits unrefrigerated, a surveillance camera with a time stamp off by hours, or a device whose software has been updated and reconfigured—each technical detail can be used to cast doubt. Defense teams and skeptical jurors ask whether evidence has been handled correctly, whether the analysis was performed according to accepted methods, and whether alternative explanations exist.

A friend of mine once told me about an elderly neighbor who was adamant about a crime she witnessed. She remembered the color of a coat, the movement of a car, the way the night smelled after rain. She was sincere to her core. Yet when asked in court if she could recognize the defendant in a lineup, she began to doubt herself. The jury watched the struggle between old certainty and present hesitation. They could have chosen to believe her—but they also had to consider whether silence in the record and the lack of confirming physical evidence created too much *reason* to doubt.

How these reasons intersect and why outcomes feel unfair

These three reasons—insufficient evidence, procedural protections, and credibility issues—do not arrive as isolated islands. They often collide. A questionable piece of evidence may be the product of an illegal search. An eyewitness's shaky memory might have been reinforced by suggestive police procedures. A confession might be powerful, but if it was obtained under duress, it cannot stand. The combination can make a strong-seeming case collapse.

For those who hoped for conviction, the outcome can feel like failure. For those defending a person, an acquittal can be a relief hard-earned through advocacy and persistence. Both reactions are human and valid. The legal system is designed with a bias toward protecting the defendant from erroneous conviction. That bias can feel like justice for one and like a travesty for another.

It helps to remember that a verdict is not a moral absolute conveyed by a single word. It is the end result of a process meant to weigh evidence, test reliability, and ensure fairness. When the process works as intended, it may protect the innocent and hold the guilty accountable. When it does not, it reveals weaknesses we must address—better investigation methods, more careful evidence handling, improved jury instructions, and ongoing legal reform.

So what can be done? Practical steps and a small hope

If you are a juror, the most important thing is to treat your role with humility. Your job is not to be a judge on the emotions of the courtroom but a careful assessor of evidence. Listen, take notes if allowed, and remember that reasonable doubt is a practical test. If the facts leave you wondering, it is okay—indeed required—to acquit.

If you are a victim, the process may feel cold and frustrating. Seek support—emotional, legal, and practical. Learn about the stages of a case so you can understand why certain evidence may be excluded. That knowledge won't make the result less painful but may help you see the system's boundaries.

If you are a prosecutor or an investigator, the lesson is clear: build strong, corroborated cases. Document procedures carefully. Train witnesses and handle evidence with meticulous care. The difference between a conviction and an acquittal can hinge on the smallest procedural step.

For defense lawyers, the work often involves pointing out what jurors already suspect: gaps, inconsistencies, and rights violations. A good defense does not just create doubt; it tells an alternate story that is coherent, believable, and grounded in facts.

And for the public, there is a broader lesson about living with a system that chooses caution over certainty. The rule that prefers acquittal when doubt remains is a moral judgment. It protects vulnerable people from the irreversible harm of wrongful punishment. It will always be frustrating to those who want clear closure. But as long as human beings are fallible, and as long as power is concentrated in the state, society must choose how to constrain that power.

A closing scene: the echo that remains

Back in that snow-damp courtroom, after the not guilty verdict, people left slowly. Some hugged, others walked out in silence. The young man who had stood trial felt both free and hollow. He had lost months of life to the process: job, reputation, the private slice of his days he could not get back. The woman who had cried came up to him in the hallway and, after a long moment, nodded. It was not a resolution; it was a pause where human beings acknowledged the fragile balances the law tries to manage.

The next morning the neighborhood had puddles and the smell of melted snow. Life resumed in the small, practical tasks of making coffee and answering emails. But the memory of that afternoon stayed with me. It reminded me that the law is lived in moments like these—tense, uncertain, and messy—but also in a commitment to a set of rules that protect people even when that protection is costly.

Not guilty verdicts are not mysteries to be solved by outrage alone. They are outcomes of standards, procedures, and human judgments. They teach us about the limits of proof, the importance of rights, and the delicate ways credibility is built and broken. Understanding those reasons does not make every outcome comfortable. But it does give us a clearer view of why the justice system acts the way it does—and how we might act to make it better.

Chapter 4

When "Not Guilty" Means More Than a Verdict

Subtittle: Types of Legal Defenses Used to Achieve Not Guilty

The first time I walked into a courtroom that felt like it could swallow a life, the lights were too bright and the air too still. A fan rattled somewhere in the ceiling. People shuffled paper and kept their heads down. I remember thinking then that trials are, at their core, stories — stories about what happened, why it happened, and whether it should have happened at all. The phrase "not guilty" is often treated like a binary outcome: win or lose. But behind that two-word verdict is a map of strategies, human choices, and, sometimes, the narrowest margins between punishment and freedom.

This chapter traces three of the most common ways defendants reach a not guilty verdict: *self-defense and justified actions*, *alibi and witness testimony*, and *lack of intent or knowledge*. I'll walk each of these through scenes you can see and feel — the flash of a panic-struck hand, an overheard phone call that becomes an alibi, the quiet unraveling of intent where the accused simply didn't know what they were doing. These are not legal forms you file; they are narratives assembled in public, in front of juries, guided by rules and human judgment.

How defenses are stories — and why that matters

Before we get to the specifics, a small, stubborn truth: the law wants facts, but humans make meaning out of facts. A defense lawyer doesn't just hand a judge a legal theory; they construct a story that makes the defendant's actions understandable, believable, and defensible. That story must fit within the rules of evidence and the language of the law. It must also connect: jurors need to see themselves in the moment the defendant faced. That is why sensory detail, timing, and motive matter. A shaking voice on the stand or a dirty kitchen light that flickered during the incident can be more persuasive than pages of statute.

With that in mind, let's sit with three core defenses, each a different way of saying, "What happened was not a crime—or not this person's fault."

Self-Defense and Justified Actions

There is an old photograph I come back to in my mind: a small storefront at dusk. Rain beads on the awning, and the shopkeeper, a woman in her fifties, is standing in the doorway with her hands full of receipts and a cigarette. A man lunges toward the cash register. The shopkeeper shoves him away, he falls, and later she is charged. The legal issue is not whether she shoved him — it is whether she was *justified* in using force to protect her property or herself.

Self-defense is one of those defenses that look simple on paper and messy in reality. At the heart of it lies the idea that everyone has a right to protect themselves, their loved ones, and sometimes their property. But the law sets limits. The force used must be reasonable in the moment, proportionate to the threat, and often, where required, based on a genuine and immediate fear of harm.

There are three layers to understand here:

- The factual layer: What actually happened? Did the defendant perceive a threat? Was that perception reasonable?
- The legal layer: Did the defendant's response align with statutory rules — for example, whether retreat was required or if the jurisdiction allows "stand your ground" defenses?
- The persuasive layer: Can the jury be made to feel the urgency, fear, or confusion the defendant experienced?

Consider a hypothetical I once heard described by a public defender: late at night, a woman walking home hears footsteps behind her. They quicken. She turns and sees a figure reach into his pocket. She lashes out, and the man falls and later claims excessive force. In court, her attorney does not start with rules. He starts by recreating the scene: the halo of the streetlight, the echo of heels, the smell of wet pavement. He invites the jury to remember a time they felt alone and frightened. That is the persuasive move. Once the jury has felt it, the legal elements — imminence, reasonableness, proportionality — slide into place more easily.

Self-defense is not only about fear of bodily harm. Some jurisdictions allow defense of property, defense of others, and even defense of the home as distinct doctrines. There are caveats, though. Use of deadly force, for example, is generally justified only when the defendant reasonably believed they faced a threat of death or serious bodily harm. And if a defendant was the initial aggressor, claiming self-defense will be much harder unless they can show they tried to withdraw from the fight and communicated that withdrawal.

Stories that succeed in court often hinge on small human details: a visible bruise, a torn shirt, a neighbor's testimony that the victim had a pattern of violent behavior. These details create a chain from perception to action that jurors can follow without inventing motives.

Alibi and Witness Testimonies

In the corner of the same courthouse, another case unfolds: a man sits calmly while his watch — the small silver thing he checks unconsciously — becomes an unlikely hero. He claims he was miles away when the crime occurred, and his sister's text messages, surveillance footage from a grocery store, and a time-stamped ride-hail receipt become the threads of his alibi.

An alibi is one of the most straightforward defenses in theory: if you can show you weren't present, you could not have committed the act. In practice, alibis live or die on credibility and detail.

Two truths about alibis stand out. First, they must be specific. "I was home all night" is fragile. "I was at 7-Eleven at 10:14 p.m., paid with a card, then walked into my sister's apartment at 10:32 p.m." — that becomes tangible. Second, corroboration matters. Corroboration can come from digital traces (camera footage, phone location, receipts), independent witnesses, or physical evidence.

Witness testimony is a double-edged sword. A reliable witness can make an alibi shine; an unreliable witness can collapse it. Juries are asked to judge not just what witnesses say but how they say it. Memory is a pliable thing; the same person can be honest yet mistaken. That is why defense teams spend hours prepping alibi witnesses: rehearsing timelines, reminding them of small sensory anchor points that make recollection real. Did the store play a song that night? Was there a particular cashier with a tattoo? These tiny details can tip a witness from vague to credible.

There is also a drama inherent in cross-examination. Prosecutors will look for motives to lie — family ties, financial incentives, grudges. Defense attorneys must anticipate and mitigate those attacks. They do this by lining up multiple, independent alibi supports: phone records, CCTV, non-family witnesses, timestamps. The more different kinds of evidence point to the same picture, the less room there is for the prosecution's story to breathe.

I recall a composite of several cases in which alibis were defeated not because the defendant was lying, but because human schedules are messy. Late dinners, traffic delays, and delayed receipts created gaps that a careful prosecutor exploited. That is a caution: an alibi must be built like a bridge, with supports at every point.

Lack of Intent or Knowledge of the Crime

Perhaps the quietest, most conceptual defense is the claim that the defendant simply did not *intend* to commit a crime — or did not *know* they were doing something criminal. Many crimes require a *mental state* — a requirement that the defendant acted knowingly, intentionally, recklessly, or negligently. Without that mental state, a person might have performed the same act but not satisfied the elements of the crime.

This defense plays out in many shapes. Consider a young man who signs for a package he thinks is his neighbor's. Inside is contraband. He is charged with possession. His defense? He did not know the package contained illegal items. Or consider someone who pushes through a crowd and is later accused of battery. If the shove was accidental, without intent to harm, then there is no criminal intent.

Proving lack of intent is often about context. What did the defendant *believe* at the time? What did they *know*? Judges and juries are asked to reach back into a mind at a moment in time, a notoriously slippery task. Lawyers will use character evidence, patterns of behavior, and ordinary life details to paint a plausible internal state: a person who has no history with drugs is less likely to have known about contraband; a pharmacist is more likely to understand the contents of a bottle than a layperson.

I once heard about a defense team that built a case around an everyday mistake. Their client, an elderly man, had been accused of failing to file certain tax forms. He had been a small-business owner who lost his wife the year before and had been handling unfamiliar online filings for the first time. His explanation — that he was overwhelmed and confused — might sound weak to some, but when paired with medical records showing recent cognitive decline, testimony from his CPA, and an honest expression of remorse, the lack-of-intent argument gained weight. It was not a get-out-of-jail-free story; it was a human story about mistakes, limitations, and the law's requirement that intention matters.

There are limits. Some offenses are strict liability crimes — think certain public safety violations — where the law does not require proof of intent. In those rare instances, lack of intent won't succeed. But for most serious crimes, intent and knowledge are central, and undermining them can be decisive.

How these defenses are litigated: the human work

All three defenses — self-defense, alibi, lack of intent — require more than legal citations. They require preparation, empathy, and attention to detail. Defense teams do what storytellers do: they seek witnesses, anchor facts with sensory detail, and anticipate counter-narratives.

Preparation looks like this in the real world: hours interviewing clients to pull out not just what happened but how it felt; subpoenaing phone records and surveillance footage; visiting the scene to understand sight lines and sounds; talking to bystanders who might have seen a face or not; preparing clients to testify under cross-examination so they don't sound evasive or robotic.

Empathy is essential because defendants are often embarrassed, angry, or detached. A good lawyer finds a way to coax a human voice from someone whose stress makes them sound flinty. A juror needs to believe in the defendant as a person, not as a label.

And detail matters. In one case, a defense hinged on the pattern of a kitchen light that flickered at the moment an alleged assault occurred. The light made a witness second-guess what they'd seen. A defense investigator found a long, unpaid electric bill and an old bulb. Small facts like that can nudge a jury toward reasonable doubt.

When defenses overlap — and the dance of strategy

Often, these defenses are not exclusive. A defendant might claim they were not present (alibi) and that, even if they were present, they acted in self-defense. Or they might argue lack of intent while also producing an alibi witness as a backup. The choice of which defenses to present in court is a strategic one. Some defenses require the defendant to testify; others can be offered entirely through witnesses and physical evidence. Whether to put a client on the stand depends on whether their testimony would help more than it might harm.

Counsel must also weigh the jury's likely perceptions. Juries are a cross-section of people with different life experiences. In some communities, claims of self-defense resonate, especially where crime feels like a daily threat. In others, an alibi reinforced by digital evidence like timestamps and GPS is more persuasive.

A wise defense attorney listens to the client but does not simply echo their instinct. Lawyers translate lived experience into a frame jurors can accept. That sometimes means reshaping the narrative, highlighting particular moments, and letting others fall into the background. It is not deceit; it is selection and emphasis — the same work historians do when choosing which facts to foreground in a story.

What "not guilty" actually saves — and doesn't

A not guilty verdict returns freedom. It prevents the state from punishing someone for that crime. But it does not necessarily erase consequences outside the courtroom. Arrest records, public suspicion, and the memories of those involved can linger. People talk about acquittal as a clean break, and sometimes it is. Other times, it is simply the end point of a story that will continue in different forms — social pain, lost jobs, fractured relationships.

There is also a moral complexity. For victims, a not guilty verdict can feel like an injustice, even if the legal system followed its rules. For defendants, a guilty verdict can feel catastrophic, even if the person believes they acted in a way any reasonable person would under the circumstances. The criminal justice system tries to translate messy human lives into legal categories, and that friction is where many of these defenses are born.

A small scene that pulls these threads together

Imagine a summer night in a suburban kitchen. Two families live in semi-detached houses separated by a thin fence. Music drifts over the backyards. A late argument in one home spills outside. Someone witnesses a shove, a fall, and later, a charge of assault. The defendant is the younger sibling who claims he only tried to separate the fighters. The prosecution paints him as an aggressor; the defense says he acted to protect. The defendant's phone places him at a nearby laundromat for part of the evening — an alibi that seems to contradict the physical evidence. Then a neighbor remembers seeing a third person, not the defendant, with blood on their shirt. The trial becomes a web: self-defense, alibi, and lack of intent all interweaving.

In that trial, a juror might find reasonable doubt: perhaps the defendant had tried to stop the fight but stepped in wrong; perhaps the timeline was compressed; perhaps the wound on the victim was not from the defendant's hand. The not guilty verdict would not be a declaration of moral innocence for everyone involved. It would say simply that the state did not meet its burden to prove guilt beyond a reasonable doubt. That standard is high by design. It is the fulcrum on which liberty rests.

Closing: what to take away from these defenses

If there is a single practical takeaway, it is this: the law is practical, human, and procedural. Winning a not guilty verdict does not require magical truths; it requires preparation, narrative coherence, and attention to human detail.

- For self-defense, the crucial elements are the defendant's honest perception of danger and the reasonableness of their response.
- For alibis, specificity and corroboration turn vague claims into strong narratives.
- For lack of intent or knowledge, the task is to make the defendant's mental state plausible and to show how the law demands more than mere action.

These defenses also teach us about humility. They remind us that life happens quickly and unpredictably and that the law is a collective attempt to slow things down and ask: *what did you know, and why did you do it?* In the rooms where those questions are argued, lawyers are less like chess players and more like translators, turning lived moments — the sudden shove, the muffled phone alarm, the blank stare of a person who did not mean harm — into a story a jury can accept.

When the verdict comes — when "not guilty" is read — it is not an end of human complexity. It is a momentary closure in a long human story. For the counsel who built the narrative, it is confirmation that facts, feeling, and law can be woven together. For the rest of us, it is a reminder that justice depends not just on rules written on paper, but on the care with which we tell each other's stories.

Chapter 5

The Role of Evidence in Securing a Not Guilty Ruling

I remember the first time I watched a courtroom pivot on a single vial of blood. It was a small courthouse, late afternoon light angling through high windows, and the prosecution's DNA expert had come across as steady and confident. The defense attorney, a woman with quiet patience, asked a handful of slow questions about how the sample had been stored. The expert's answers started precise, then frayed. By the time she stood down, jurors were leaning forward as if the air in the room had become thinner. The not-guilty verdict that followed felt less like a surprise and more like the logical end of a moment when evidence stopped being absolute and became human — incomplete, contingent, and open to doubt.

Evidence sits at the center of criminal trials. It is the scaffolding on which stories are built: who did what, when, and where. But there is a difference between the *idea* of evidence as flawless fact and the messy reality of how evidence is collected, processed, and presented. That distance — between what evidence appears to be and what it can prove — is where acquittals are won. This chapter walks through that terrain: the power of DNA, fingerprints, and physical evidence; the craft of cross-examination to undermine reliability; and the crucial ability to exclude evidence that was improperly obtained. Together, these are the levers a defense lawyer uses to turn uncertainty into reasonable doubt.

Why DNA, Fingerprints, and Physical Evidence Matter — and Why They Don't Always Decide a Case

When people hear "forensic evidence," they often imagine a mix of bright lights, lab coats, and incontestable science. DNA has, until recently, been the holy grail of that image — tiny biological traces translated into near-unique genetic profiles. Fingerprints are portrayed as even simpler: distinct whorls and lines that point to one person. Physical evidence — a weapon, a footprint, a fiber — provides the sensory anchor that makes a story feel real in a jury's ears.

But every piece of evidence has limits. DNA may be compelling, but it depends on context. Was the DNA from a primary transfer or secondary contact? How much DNA was present? Was the profile partial or mixtures of multiple contributors? Fingerprint identification rests on pattern comparison, which involves subjective judgment. A partial print found at a scene might *resemble* the defendant's print, but resemblance is not the same as certainty. Physical evidence ties a person to a place or object, but it rarely tells the whole story. A gun at a scene might be owned by someone else, or a fiber might have transferred days earlier.

The practical danger comes when jurors equate the presence of scientific evidence with *proof beyond a reasonable doubt*. As an attorney, part of the job is to remind the fact-finder that science in practice is vulnerable to human error, contamination, misinterpretation, and laboratory limits. A vial of blood does not speak for itself; it carries a history. It was collected by a person, packaged by a technician, processed by a machine run by another person. Each step is an opportunity for error.

I once sat through testimony from a forensic lab technician who described how small the swabs were that they used. He held one up and squinted at it under the courtroom light. Later, a photograph of the packaging came into evidence showing a tiny tear in a corner. That small tear, which might have escaped notice in a sterile report, became central: how could we be confident that the sample had remained untouched from collection to testing? That doubt was enough to erode the apparent certainty of the DNA match.

Cross-Examination: The Art of Turning Science Into Story

Cross-examination is not about humiliating the witness; it's about revealing the limits of their certainty in a way that ordinary people can follow. To challenge forensic evidence effectively, you translate lab procedures into commonsense questions. You slow the expert down and make each step of the chain visible to jurors.

Start by establishing context. Ask the expert to describe, in plain language, how the evidence moved from the scene to the lab. Where was it stored at each moment? Who touched it? What protective measures were used? These questions do a lot of work because they show that evidence has a history, and histories have friction. When an expert is pushed to explain the *probability* of contamination, or to quantify the chance of an erroneous match, jurors can begin to weigh the strength of the claim instead of accepting it as absolute.

Then move to specifics: laboratory protocols, validation studies, and error rates. Not every juror needs to understand polymerase chain reaction cycles or probabilistic genotyping. What they do need to understand is whether the technique used is generally accepted and whether it's been properly validated in the lab that processed the sample. Questions like, "How often has your lab run this test and gotten inconsistent results?" or "Have independent studies shown this method to be reliable with samples this small?" convert scientific certainty into testable assertions.

One tactic that works again and again is the *comparison to everyday experience*. When a fingerprint examiner claims a match, ask how many matching points are required and whether any of those points were smudged or incomplete. When a DNA analyst claims a match on a mixed sample, ask whether the presence of another person's DNA could obscure or shift the interpretation. These are simple questions, but they force the witness to tie abstract expert assertions back to the physical, imperfect world jurors inhabit.

A cross-examination must also expose institutional factors: staffing levels at the lab, backlogs, and training. If a lab is overwhelmed or underfunded, mistakes become more probable. Ask whether the analyst followed the lab's own protocols, and get the analyst to acknowledge whether deviations were documented. When an expert admits that a certain step was skipped or that documentation is missing, the illusion of flawless science cracks.

Finally, there's the tone. The best cross-examinations are precise and calm. They allow the expert to deny or qualify, and then they take the concessions and build them into a simple, memorable narrative for the jury: the evidence may point *toward* the defendant, but it does not *prove* the defendant's guilt beyond a reasonable doubt.

Contamination, Error, and the Chain of Custody: Where Science Breaks Down

Science depends on control. Control means keeping variables limited and processes repeatable. The crime scene is the opposite of a controlled laboratory. It's chaotic — weather, pedestrians, first responders, and time all conspire to contaminate places and things. Chain of custody rules exist because of this reality. They are the record of who handled the evidence and when, and breaks in that chain are often fatal for the prosecution's claim of integrity.

When preparing to challenge evidence, the defense looks for gaps: missing logs, unlabeled items, inconsistent dates, or instances where evidence was left in unsecured storage. These gaps provide the factual basis for arguing that contamination or misidentification is not only possible but reasonably likely.

Laboratory error is another vulnerability. Even the most careful labs make mistakes: sample mislabeling, mixing during analysis, clerical errors. Sometimes these errors are systemic — poor oversight, reliance on outdated procedures, or inadequate validation of new software. At other times they're human: a tired technician misreads a label late at night. Cross-examination should make these possibilities tangible. Ask whether the lab performs blind proficiency tests. Ask how many staff members sign off at each stage. Ask whether the lab uses audits and whether any prior issues have been documented.

A practical anecdote: a defense team once obtained a shipment manifest showing that two different cases' samples had been packed together during transit. The prosecution had no immediate answer. The jury didn't need to be told that this made a swap impossible; they only needed to see that the possibility of a mix-up existed. The reasonable doubt was born in the space between possibility and proof.

Challenging the Reliability of New and Old Forensic Methods

Not all forensic techniques are created equal. Some have decades of research and validation behind them; others are relatively new and less tested. Courts have borrowed from scientific gatekeeping principles to decide whether expert testimony is admissible. In federal courts, the Daubert standard requires judges to act as gatekeepers, looking at whether a method has been tested, peer-reviewed, has known error rates, and is generally accepted in the relevant scientific community (Daubert v. Merrell Dow Pharmaceuticals, 1993). State courts vary, but the question is largely the same: is the method reliable here?

Defense lawyers must do homework. If a method is new — for example, a proprietary statistical algorithm used to interpret complex DNA mixtures — the defense should probe the software's validation, the peer-reviewed support for the algorithm, and the transparency of its methods. When a method is old but unscientific — like certain forms of bite-mark analysis — the defense should highlight peer-reviewed critiques and error studies.

A courtroom scene I keep returning to involved a lab that used an automated system to call DNA contributors from weak mixtures. The analyst testified to high confidence. On cross, the defense brought a published study showing that the system had inflated match probabilities in low-template samples. The judge admitted the system's results but allowed the defense to place the study before the jury. The jury's job was now clearer: weighing a machine's confident claim against independent research that said the machine could be overconfident. The result? Reasonable doubt.

Excluding Improperly Obtained Evidence: The Gateway to Acquittal

Sometimes the most effective tactic isn't to attack the science but to keep the evidence out entirely. Constitutional protections against unreasonable searches and seizures are a defense attorney's most powerful tool. If evidence is obtained in violation of the Fourth Amendment, courts may exclude it under the exclusionary rule. This is not just a technicality; it changes the entire narrative available to a jury.

Challenges to admissibility often start before trial. A motion to suppress asks the court to find that law enforcement lacked probable cause, exceeded a warrant, or acted without a valid warrant when evidence was seized. These hearings are opportunities to examine police reports, bodycam footage, dispatch logs, and the sequence of events. If police conduct strays from constitutional limits — for example, a prolonged stop without reasonable suspicion, a warrantless search of a home, or an interrogative that lacked proper Miranda warnings — a judge can rule that the evidence must be excluded.

Even where police acted in good faith, procedural errors matter. Illegally obtained confessions remain powerful; jurors give them weight. Excluding a confession can deflate the prosecution's entire case. Likewise, if the chain of custody is broken, or the seizure itself was unlawful, physical evidence can be suppressed.

There are limitations. Courts sometimes apply exceptions, like the inevitable discovery doctrine or the good-faith exception to warrant defects. Yet these doctrines do not swallow the rule. Persistent, precise challenges can succeed, particularly when the defense frames violations as unnecessary departures from standard police procedure rather than unavoidable mistakes.

Strategy in Concert: How Evidence, Cross-Examination, and Exclusion Work Together

A trial is a story contest. The prosecution offers a plot built around evidence; the defense has three tasks: destabilize key facts, suggest alternative explanations, and remind the jury of reasonable doubt. These tasks overlap across the three tools we've discussed.

Imagine a robbery case where the prosecution's strongest evidence is a latent fingerprint on a cash register and a partial DNA match on a discarded glove. A comprehensive defense strategy might begin with a motion to suppress any items obtained through a questionable search of the defendant's car. Parallel to that, the defense would investigate the lab that processed the glove and the fingerprint. Cross-examination would focus on how the print was lifted, whether it was complete, and the examiner's subjective thresholds. For the DNA, the defense would probe the sample's size, whether mixture analysis was properly validated, and whether the lab's software could overstate a match. Each attack — admissibility, reliability, chain of custody — reinforces the others. If the glove is suppressed, the fingerprint stands alone and loses weight. If the lab's method is shown to be unreliable, both forensic anchors weaken.

These overlapping strategies are often not dramatic in a single courtroom moment. They are accumulative. Jurors make decisions by degrees, not by sudden conversions. The goal is to make the prosecution's story brittle enough that a reasonable doubt remains.

Ethics and the Limits of Doubt

A final, necessary note on ethics: challenging evidence is not about manufacturing doubt where none exists. It's about ensuring that the fact-finder understands the real limits of the proof offered against an individual. Good defense lawyers respect this boundary. They aim to reveal uncertainty, not to invent it. When evidence is solid, cross-examination should be proportionate and fair. When evidence is weak, advocacy must be relentless.

There are also pragmatic limits. Not every flawed procedure leads to suppression. Not every lab error is fatal. But a disciplined approach — meticulous document review, targeted motions, and patient, lucid cross-examination — increases the chance that a jury will see uncertainty where the prosecution hoped they would see fact.

A Quiet Victory: What a Not Guilty Ruling Feels Like

The not-guilty verdict I mentioned at the start did not feel like the triumph you see in movies. There were no shouts, only a slow exhale from the family members in the back and a quiet handshake in the defense table. The defense attorney later told me she had not aimed to tear apart the DNA evidence completely. She had focused on three things: the chain of custody, a lab that had recently suffered technician turnover, and the prosecutor's reliance on an overconfident match probability. By the time she finished, the jury didn't have to choose between two competing absolute truths. They only had to decide whether the prosecution had met the high burden of proof. They decided it had not.

What you take from a rule like that is not simply a court transcript or a check of boxes; it's a reminder that the legal system is not a machine that converts traces into inevitabilities. It's a human institution that depends on standards, careful procedure, and honest presentation. Scientific evidence can be decisive, but only when it is handled with rigor and humility. When it is not, when human error or procedural shortcuts enter the picture, juries — when properly guided — will withhold conviction.

Takeaways and Practice

If you leave this chapter with one practical idea, let it be this: treat evidence as a narrative full of moments where human decisions mattered. Follow the path from the scene to the lab. Ask who touched the item, when, and how. Probe the lab's validation studies and staffing. Demand transparency from automated systems. And when constitutional protections have been compromised, pursue exclusion with the same rigor you apply to cross-examination.

The courtroom is where doubt becomes a decisive force. It is not about winning by trickery but about insisting that claims of certainty meet the real-world standards that science and law both require. When evidence ceases to be a crystal-clear window into the past and becomes a set of plausible but contestable facts, reasonable doubt returns as the right, and often the only, outcome.

Chapter 6

Case Studies of Not Guilty Verdicts

The courtroom had a way of holding its breath. Chairs creaked. Cameras clicked. People who had been strangers for months leaned forward as if they could catch the verdict by sheer will. I remember watching one televised moment when the foreperson cleared their throat and spoke two words that would change everything: *not guilty.* The room exhaled in waves—sobs, laughter, silence. For some, it was relief so raw it looked like grief. For others, it felt like a failure of the system. Those two words are simple, but their echoes are complicated.

This chapter collects a handful of high-profile not guilty verdicts and exonerations. These are not checklists of legal maneuvers. They are stories about people, about choices made in the hum of pretrial rooms and in the hush of jury selection, about tactics that worked and mistakes that taught bitter lessons. Each case is its own world. Taken together, they show patterns: the power of narrative, the weakness of shoddy evidence, and the stubborn human cost of error.

Amanda Knox — The Weapon of Story

I picture a crowded Italian courtroom lit by a clinical light that seemed to strip people of privacy. Amanda Knox was young and foreign in an environment that translated every misstep into suspicion. Her case became shorthand for something larger: how a person's demeanor can be turned against them. Prosecutors framed behavior, notes, and inconsistencies as a neat narrative of guilt. That narrative held until the weaker pieces—questionable forensic links, unreliable witness statements—started to unspool.

The successful legal strategies in Amanda Knox's final acquittal were not about dramatic last-minute evidence. They were patient: methodical challenges to how evidence had been collected and interpreted, insistence on the limits of what the DNA could actually show, and a steady reminder that *circumstance does not equal guilt.* Her defense attorneys pushed back against the narrative, forced forensic review, and highlighted the cultural misunderstandings that had made certain behaviors seem incriminating when they were not. The Italian Supreme Court's final decision — that the evidence did not support the narrative of guilt — underscores a basic truth: where story outruns proof, the law must step in. Source: BBC News; The New York Times.

The lesson here is painfully human. Jurors are not blank slates. They bring stories. A defense that ignores the narratives forming outside the courtroom—media portrayals, public anger, stereotypes—hands the prosecution half its case. The remedy is twofold: attack weak science and replace the prosecution's story with a plausible, humane alternative. That means crafting a narrative where the defendant is a full person, not just a suspect on a poster.

O.J. Simpson — The Power of Doubt and the Spotlight

If you were alive in the mid-1990s, you remember the television. The O.J. Simpson trial was a parade of spectacle: slow-speed chases, celebrity witnesses, and a nation split into living rooms and water-cooler debates. But beneath the cameras was a defense strategy that was cold and simple: create reasonable doubt and exploit institutional distrust.

Simpson's legal team understood the room. They knew jurors' mistrust of the police would be as powerful as any piece of physical evidence. So they focused on showing how evidence could have been contaminated, how procedures might have been botched, and how motive and context could be read differently. They leaned into a larger, uncomfortable social history—questioning police credibility in a way that resonated with many jurors. Whether you agree with the verdict or not, the legal tactics were precise: relentless cross-examination, meticulous attention to chain-of-custody questions, and an unflinching focus on the rule that the state must prove its case beyond reasonable doubt. Source: PBS Frontline; The New York Times.

There's an important, nuanced takeaway here. Doubt is not the same as truth. A defense can win by showing doubt and still be wrong about what *actually* happened. But the justice system is built on a standard that favors caution. The strategy worked because the defense found seams in the prosecution's fabric and tugged until the whole thing came apart in jurors' minds.

Casey Anthony — Narrative vs. Proof

In a Florida courtroom in 2011, the verdict in the Casey Anthony trial split the public into two tribes: those who saw justice, and those who saw an escape. The case hinged on the disappearance and death of a child, which is to say it swam in a fog of emotion from the start. For the defense, the path to not guilty was straightforward in form if not in feeling: point out the lack of definitive proof linking the accused to the crime, and highlight plausible alternative explanations.

Casey Anthony's defense did not have to construct a heroic narrative. It had to dismantle the prosecution's claims piece by piece—questioning forensic timelines, pointing out gaps in direct evidence, and reminding jurors that emotional intensity does not substitute for proof. In juries deciding high-emotion cases, dispassionate emphasis on standards of proof can be the decisive factor. Source: CNN; The New York Times.

What this case teaches is stark but necessary. Not guilty does not equal moral innocence in the public's eyes. It means the prosecution failed to meet the legal bar. For defense attorneys, the practical art is not just in attacking evidence; it is in keeping a jury's emotions from outrunning their reason. That is a delicate, often thankless task.

The Central Park Five — Exoneration by Truth and the Cost of Confession Coercion

The story of the Central Park Five is less about a single courtroom win and more about the slow, halting path from conviction to exoneration. Five teenagers were convicted in a frenzy of panic and racial tension; their confessions—later shown to have been coerced—were central to the prosecution. Years later, DNA evidence and a confession by another man led to vacated convictions and a formal exoneration.

This case exposes two brutal truths about how wrongful convictions take hold. First, aggressive interrogation tactics, especially with vulnerable youths, can manufacture confessions that feel like facts to juries. Second, once a criminal narrative is set, it is stubborn. The legal strategies that eventually succeeded were not quick courtroom theatrics. They were patient, forensic re-examination and the relentless work of advocates who refused to let the original story stand unchallenged. Public pressure, new technology, and tenacity combined to correct what had gone wrong. Source: The New York Times; When They See Us (documentary).

There is a narrow human detail that often gets lost in case summaries: the teenagers themselves spent years carrying the weight of a guilt that was not theirs. Exoneration came with relief, but also with scars—lost adolescence, reputations that never fully recovered. The lesson is both legal and moral. Systems must protect the vulnerable during interrogation. Defense counsel, when representing young clients, must not only object in court but also guard them from the room where silence can be broken into a false confession.

Rubin "Hurricane" Carter — The Role of Advocacy and New Evidence

Rubin Carter's name carries a different kind of story. A boxer whose life became intertwined with song and activism, Carter saw his convictions overturned after decades behind bars. His case is a study in how legal delay and public advocacy can intersect with law to correct injustice.

Carter's legal team eventually exposed prosecutorial misconduct and weaknesses in the initial investigations. The legal victory was built on demonstrating that the original case had been corrupted by errors, biases, and omissions. But it was also the product of relentless advocacy: journalists, musicians, and legal advocates kept his name in the light until new legal arguments could be pressed. Source: The New York Times; legal history reviews.

Carter's exoneration offers a clear lesson: legal systems are not self-correcting in the short term. Sometimes, a case needs an outside chorus—reporters, artists, citizens—to keep pressure on institutions. That kind of pressure can be uncomfortable, but it can also bring forgotten facts back into the room where they belong.

West Memphis Three — Pleas, Publicity, and the Limits of Closure

The West Memphis Three were teenagers convicted in a case marked by sensationalism and shaky evidence. Years later, new DNA testing did not point to them, and they were released after entering Alford pleas—an uneasy legal device where defendants maintain innocence while conceding that prosecutors have enough evidence to convict.

Their release illustrates a complex legal reality. The Alford plea offered a way out without the state conceding error outright. For the men, it was a pragmatic path to freedom; for many observers, it was an unsatisfying moral compromise. The case underscores how the law sometimes trades absolute truth for practical resolution. Source: Rolling Stone; PBS Frontline.

Here the lesson is about limits. Even successful defense work that ends in freedom can leave open questions. Defense attorneys may secure release but also face the choice between a guaranteed exit and the risk of retrial. The lesson for future defenders is to weigh legal freedom against moral clarity—and to recognize that sometimes victory will be partial.

What Successful Defense Tactics Tend to Share

Across these cases, certain defense tactics recur. They are not magic spells, but they are reliable tools when wielded well.

- Story over scatter: Successful defenses craft a coherent alternative narrative. The prosecution presents a story of what happened. The defense doesn't simply deny; it offers context, motive, and plausible alternatives that make the prosecution's version less certain.
- Forensics are fragile: Science is a star in courtrooms, but it is also misused. The best defenses know the limits of forensic evidence and bring in their own experts to test the prosecution's claims. Chain-of-custody questions, contamination risk, and method limitations are often decisive battlegrounds.
- Jury work: A jury is not an algorithm. Selecting jurors who can apply the law without being overwhelmed by media or emotion is critical. Once seated, jurors must be addressed not as a legal robot but as human beings who need a clear story and a calm standard: reasonable doubt.
- Process and procedure: Many wrongful convictions rest on procedural errors—botched lineups, coerced confessions, improper searches. A thorough defense uses motions and filings to expose these problems early and often.
- Patience and pressure: Some resolutions come only after years of work. Appeals, new testing, and public advocacy can all be part of the toolkit. Lawyers who see cases as marathons, not sprints, can sometimes outwait error.

Lessons That Reach Beyond Lawyers

These cases offer lessons that go beyond tactics. They teach us about fairness, narrative, and the social forces that shape guilt and innocence.

First, the justice system is formal but human. Procedural safeguards exist for a reason: to prevent the terrible finality of wrongful punishment. When those safeguards are ignored or weakened, the consequences are lifelong.

Second, public opinion can be both helpful and harmful. Media attention helped free some wrongfully convicted people; in other cases it warped perceptions and increased pressure to secure convictions. Lawyers must manage media with care—sometimes it can be an ally, sometimes an enemy.

Third, we must be humble about certainty. For jurors, the lesson is not that the system is perfect. It's that the legal standard—beyond reasonable doubt—is intentionally high because the cost of error is high. Not guilty sometimes equals innocent, sometimes equals lack of proof. Recognizing that ambiguity is part of civic maturity.

Finally, these stories show the cost of rushed judgments. Whether a jury is swayed by a dramatic confession, a persuasive prosecutor, or a viral headline, the speed of judgment can be the enemy of accuracy. The defense's role is to slow things down, to force a pause where evidence can be tested against story.

A Quiet Moment and a Final Thought

After a verdict, the courthouse often empties in two kinds of silence. There's the mechanical hush of people putting on coats, and there's a softer silence—people taking in news that will change their lives. I once sat in a hallway beside a man whose trial had ended a decade earlier. He told me, quietly, that even after exoneration, he woke up some nights convinced he had lost time he would never get back. That lingering harm is the true measure of these cases.

Not guilty verdicts and exonerations teach us about the limits of proof and the resilience of hope. They remind us that law is an imperfect human endeavor and that careful, compassionate defense work protects not only individuals but the integrity of a system. When defense tactics succeed—through evidence scrutiny, narrative work, patient appeals, or public advocacy—they do more than win a case. They restore a portion of what was taken: time, reputation, dignity.

If there is an actionable takeaway for readers, it is this: demand rigor. In courts and in public life, insist that claims be tested, that confessions be scrutinized, and that forensic science be used honestly. Stories make meaning; evidence makes truth. When the two are kept in balance, the scale of justice tips where it should.

Source notes: Specific case details referenced here draw on contemporary reporting and documentary accounts, including The New York Times, BBC News, CNN, PBS Frontline, Rolling Stone, and the documentary works covering these cases.

Chapter 7

Impact of Not Guilty Verdicts on Defendants' Lives

The judge says, "Not guilty." The words land like rain on a parched field—relief at first, then the slow, stubborn work of trying to make anything grow again.

For most of us, a courtroom scene ends when the verdict is read. For the person who has been accused, arrested, and hauled into a legal drama, the story does not end there. A not guilty verdict is a legal exoneration, but it is rarely an emotional full stop. The rest of the world—friends, employers, strangers on social media, and sometimes the defendant themselves—keeps turning pages. This chapter follows what happens after the verdict: the emotional wreckage that lingers, the complicated legal and practical realities that arrive with the paperwork, and the long, often quiet work of rebuilding a life and reputation.

The first hour after acquittal is raw

Walk out of a courthouse after a not guilty verdict and you'll see the swirl of reactions. People hug. Lawyers breathe. Reporters scribble. For the defendant, the first rush is often relief so profound it feels physical—an animal uncoiling after danger has passed. But that relief can be tangled with other things: numbness, anger, shame, even a sense of unreality.

These aren't just poetic reactions. The body remembers. Months of stress change sleeping patterns, appetite, and the brain's wiring for fear and trust. People who survive traumatic legal ordeals report symptoms similar to those who survive other kinds of trauma: trouble sleeping, intrusive thoughts, panic in crowded places, and flashbacks to the worst days. Clinical research links traumatic legal experiences to symptoms of post-traumatic stress and depression. *The courtroom becomes part of the memory that won't go away* (Source: American Psychological Association).

I once spoke with Anna—a composite of several people I've met over the years—who had been accused of a crime she didn't commit. When she left court, family members cheered, but she couldn't stand the sound of applause. It brought her back to the months of interrogation and the nights she spent awake, worrying. She felt safe and unsafe at the same time: safe because the case was over, unsafe because she had been exposed, judged, and almost marked. For weeks she flinched whenever a car slowed outside her house. *She had been cleared, but her nervous system had not been told that.*

The process of being accused often involves humiliation, loss of privacy, and a feeling of being exposed. Even when the legal system declares innocence, the emotional fallout remains. Defendants may struggle with identity—wondering whether the accusation reflects something true about them despite the verdict. Many report a lingering anxiety that the same thing could happen again, a vigilance that drains energy and prevents closeness in relationships.

Guilt, even when innocent

There is another shade of feeling that is hard to anticipate: a sort of survivor guilt. People who are found not guilty sometimes feel guilty about the people who were dragged into the mess with them—their loved ones, who lost time and money fighting, or even the public officials whose reputations may have been harmed by the prosecution. They may grieve the version of their life that was interrupted. The sense of "I should feel happy, so why don't I?" can be isolating.

This is important: emotional distress after an acquittal is not weakness. It's human. Acknowledging it is the start of recovery.

Legal rights and future implications: what "not guilty" actually means

A not guilty verdict answers one specific question: did the prosecution, beyond a reasonable doubt, prove the defendant committed the crime as charged? It does not necessarily erase the rest of the experience. *Legally, the person is free of the criminal charge.* But legal freedom and practical freedom are different things.

First, records matter. Arrests, charges, and even the existence of a trial often leave traces in police records, court dockets, and online news. These traces can follow someone in routine background checks, résumé screenings, and casual Google searches. Some jurisdictions allow sealing or expungement of records after an acquittal; others do not or place limits on what can be removed. Because the rules vary widely, *it's essential to consult legal counsel* about options for sealing records and correcting public information (Source: National Conference of State Legislatures).

Second, collateral consequences are not limited to convicted people. An accusation alone can trigger administrative actions. For example, a professional licensing board might suspend someone's license pending investigation even if they are later acquitted. Employers may place employees on leave, and landlords might react to the mere presence of charges. For noncitizens, immigration consequences can be especially complex; an acquittal does not automatically mean there will be no immigration scrutiny. *Immigration law treats charges, convictions, and admissions differently depending on status and the specific allegations* (Source: U.S. Citizenship and Immigration Services). In short: the legal ecosystem after an acquittal is not uniform; different institutions interpret the presence of a charge in different ways.

Third, civil liability remains a possibility. A not guilty verdict in criminal court does not prevent a civil suit alleging harm—perhaps for the same underlying incident. The standards of proof are different, and the outcomes can diverge. People who thought they were done sometimes find themselves in drawn-out civil cases, insurance claims, or employment disputes.

Finally, there are practical issues that happen behind the scenes. If an accused person was detained, they may have lost time at work and income. Medical bills, legal fees, and the cost of rebuilding stability can be staggering. Criminal legal defense is expensive, and acquittal doesn't bring automatic reimbursement. While there are legal mechanisms in some places to seek compensation for wrongful arrest or malicious prosecution, those avenues are narrow and often difficult to succeed in. The financial aftermath can be a slow, nagging punishment after the legal question has been answered.

The paradox of rights and reality

Here's the paradox: legally, the state pulled its strongest card and failed to convict. But socially, the accusation has already become part of a person's record. People carry the story forward in ways that are messy, private, and public. The law gives a verdict; it rarely rewrites memory.

Rebuilding personal and professional reputation

Reputation is not a formal verdict; it is a social currency, slow to earn and fast to erode. After a not guilty verdict, the work of reclaiming a name can feel more like gardening than hammering down a nail. It takes time, steady effort, and sometimes a strategic plan.

First, there is the immediate mess: media coverage and social media. For some defendants, the story was covered widely; for others, the damage spread in local networks and private conversations. Even after acquittal, headlines and tweets that mention an arrest can linger. Images and stories can be shared in ways that remain searchable for years. That digital footprint complicates job searches, romance, community standing, and the simple human act of being known without the label attached.

Second, there are interpersonal repairs. Families, friends, and colleagues may have their own fears and judgments. Trust is frayed. Some relationships recover quickly; others do not. The patterns that led to accusations—miscommunications, old resentments, structural vulnerabilities—don't vanish with a verdict. In many cases, the real work is relational therapy: rebuilding trust through accountability, transparent communication, and consistent action.

Third, professional recovery often requires tactical steps. People may need to explain gaps in résumés, respond to background checks, or convince licensing boards to lift restrictions. Practical steps can include:

- Working with attorneys to correct online records or request expungement where possible.

- Preparing a concise, honest explanation for employers that focuses on facts and forward motion rather than raw emotion.
- Reaching out to mentors or respected figures in one's field who can vouch for character and work ethic.
- Engaging a professional reputation or public relations firm in high-profile cases.

None of these are magic bullets. They are tools—small, deliberate efforts that, over time, can change how a person is perceived.

A quiet example

Consider James, another composite. He was accused of wrongdoing while running a small consulting firm. Clients paused, colleagues whispered, and projects stalled. After he was found not guilty, James did not sprint back to business as usual. Instead, he held a meeting with his closest clients—quiet, honest, and factual. He explained what had happened, what he'd learned, and how he planned to ensure transparency going forward. He hired a part-time communications professional to manage facts on his website and to ensure that search results minimized residual stories. He volunteered for local boards and ramped up pro bono work. It took two years, but the steady accumulation of trustworthy actions changed the conversation about him. *No dramatic rebound, just persistence.*

That persistence—small acts that align words and deeds—matters. Reputation is rebuilt by consistency more than argument.

The role of community and employers

Recovery is not just an individual task. Communities and employers play an enormous role in whether people can move forward. When a workplace treats a fellow employee humanely—offering paid leave, facilitating a fair process, and supporting reintegration—people recover faster. When communities resist quick condemnation and prioritize due process, the social cost of accusation is lower.

Friends and family are also crucial. The default reaction of some is to distance themselves to avoid being entangled, but that often increases harm. Support that includes setting boundaries while maintaining care—such as offering help with childcare, housing, or legal logistics—makes a measurable difference in long-term recovery.

Practical steps people can take after acquittal

- Get medical and mental health care. Trauma doesn't disappear with a verdict. Therapy can help process the experience and rebuild a sense of safety.
- Seek legal advice about records. Ask an attorney whether arrest records, charges, or transcripts can be sealed, expunged, or corrected.
- Document expenses and harms. Keep records of lost wages, medical bills, and other costs related to the case. They may be important for civil claims or compensation petitions.
- Begin a reputation plan. Identify what you can control: your statements, your presence online, your professional output. Small, honest steps are better than grand proclamations.
- Reconnect intentionally. For family and friends, practice telling the truth in short, straightforward ways. Let people ask questions on their timetable.
- Slow down decision-making. Major purchases, partnerships, or public-facing moves made too soon after an ordeal can lead to mistakes. Give yourself time.

How systems can do better

This is not only an individual story. Courts, law enforcement, employers, and media outlets all contribute to the aftermath. There are practical reforms that could reduce the harm to people who are ultimately found not guilty:

- Better procedures for sealing records after an acquittal or dropped charges.
- Clearer guidelines from employers and licensing boards about interim measures and reinstatement after acquittal.
- Media standards for covering accusations that put a clearer emphasis on presumption of innocence and the lasting effects of headlines.

- Accessible mental health services for people who have been prosecuted, not just those who are convicted.

Change at the institutional level often requires public pressure and policy work. But even small shifts—like a local employer adopting a policy to protect non-convicted employees—can make a huge difference in individual lives.

A final, human note

A not guilty verdict is an important thing. It restores a legal status. But the real work of recovery is lived in bedrooms where sleep is fitful, in dinner tables where conversations start with "You had to go through that?" and in the quiet rebuilding of a professional life. That work is mundane and heroic in its own way: paying bills that piled up; explaining a gap in a résumé; learning to trust again.

If you know someone who has been acquitted, there are compassionate ways to show up. Listen more than you explain. Offer concrete help—run an errand, babysit, or bring a meal. Be careful with curiosity about the trial; people often relive the pain by retelling it. Ask what they need and accept that they may need time.

If you find yourself on the receiving end of a not guilty verdict, remember this: you are allowed to feel relief and fear at the same time. Healing does not follow a neat timeline. Small routine acts—sleeping regular hours, reaching out to one person, taking a walk—can be the scaffolding for greater recovery.

The law gave its answer; now life must catch up. Rebuilding after an acquittal is a process of patiently reclaiming privacy, financial stability, relationships, and a name. It is work for individuals, for their communities, and for the systems that touched their lives. It can be done, step by patient step, with honesty, help, and time.

Source notes: Clinical links between traumatic legal experiences and mental health outcomes are discussed broadly by the American Psychological Association. Practical and jurisdictional questions about record sealing and collateral consequences vary by state and are cataloged by entities such as the National Conference of State Legislatures. Immigration-related consequences for criminal charges are complex and depend on specific circumstances; consult U.S. Citizenship and Immigration Services or an immigration attorney for case-specific guidance.

Chapter 8

Myths and Misconceptions About Not Guilty Verdicts

The woman in the grocery line looked at me and said, with the kind of certainty that makes conversation feel like a verdict, "If the jury says not guilty, it must mean they were innocent." I smiled because I understood where she was coming from, and I also understood how often that belief collapses under the weight of the real world.

Words like "guilty" and "not guilty" carry moral force. They sound like final answers. They feel tidy. But the truth is messy. The legal system uses a narrow set of rules to decide whether the state proved a case. Those rules are powerful, and they are limited. They were designed more to protect fairness in a public contest than to pronounce moral truth. That difference — *between a legal outcome and what actually happened* — is the source of a thousand misunderstandings.

This chapter untangles those misunderstandings. I'll explain what a not guilty verdict does and does not mean, unpack why people get it wrong, and debunk the myths that trap our conversations about justice. Along the way I'll tell short scenes and small stories to show how these abstract ideas play out in real life.

Not Guilty ≠ Proven Innocent

The first and most common misconception is also the simplest: people hear "not guilty" and equate it with "innocent." That's a natural leap. In everyday speech, if someone says, "I'm not guilty," they usually mean they didn't do it. But in a courtroom, *not guilty* is a specific legal finding about the prosecution's case — not a declaration of factual innocence.

A not guilty verdict means the jury (or judge) found that the prosecution did not meet its burden: to prove the defendant's guilt *beyond a reasonable doubt*. That phrase is the heart of criminal law. It's a high bar by design. The idea is not to prove a negative — it's to make the state shoulder the risk of being wrong. As the Legal Information Institute at Cornell Law School explains, the constitution and long-standing legal practice make the burden of proof in criminal cases heavier than in civil cases (Source: Legal Information Institute, Cornell Law School).

Imagine a dimly lit intersection and two people arguing about whether someone ran a red light. Without a clear camera, the testimony of a shaken eyewitness might clash with a shaky alibi. A jury could decide the evidence isn't strong enough to convict. That doesn't mean every juror is certain the defendant couldn't have been the driver. It means reasonable doubt exists in the minds of at least some jurors. The law says that's where the verdict must stand.

How Trials Work: Burden, Evidence, and Reasonable Doubt

People often picture trials as forensic displays that reveal absolute truth. Movies feed that fantasy: a dramatic reveal, a confession, a final gasp of astonishment. Real trials are quieter and more procedural. Evidence can be excluded for technical reasons. Witnesses forget, lie, or misperceive. Paperwork gets lost. Prosecutors face deadlines and resource constraints. Juries are ordinary people trying to make sense of testimony and rules they've never used before.

Here's a small scene to ground that: I once sat in a municipal courtroom where a case hinged on a single witness whose memory had frayed. The man on the stand described a night that had felt like an ocean in his mind — distant, blurred, full of waves. He seemed genuine, but his details wavered under cross-examination. The prosecutor closed by asking the jurors to fill gaps with common sense. The defense closed by showing how memory twists over distance. The jury deliberated for less than an hour and returned a not guilty verdict. To an outside observer, that decision could mean different things: some jurors had doubts; others thought the evidence was too thin. The law honors the doubt.

The crucial lesson: criminal verdicts respond to how convincingly the state proves a story, not to whether the defendant did or did not do the act in some absolute sense.

Common Public Misunderstandings — and Why They Persist

Let's look at a few myths and unwind them.

Myth 1: A not guilty verdict means the defendant did not commit the act.

Reality: It means the prosecution failed to convince the jury beyond a reasonable doubt. The defendant may be factually innocent, or the evidence may simply have been weak or unavailable.

Myth 2: If someone is acquitted, the system failed.

Reality: The system is designed to avoid convicting the innocent. Sometimes that means guilty people go free because the evidence didn't meet the high burden of proof. That outcome is uncomfortable but deliberate. The legal maxim is that it's better for many guilty people to go free than for one innocent person to be wrongly punished.

Myth 3: After acquittal, the person faces no consequences.

Reality: Acquittal ends the criminal risk in many places, but it doesn't automatically erase collateral harms: reputations can be damaged, jobs lost, relationships strained. Civil liability can follow a criminal acquittal. Administrative penalties — like professional discipline or immigration consequences — may carry on separately. The legal world splits consequences across systems; an outcome in one arena doesn't wipe the slate clean in others.

Myth 4: Juries always get it right.

Reality: Juries are fallible because humans are fallible. They do their best with what they are given: instructions, evidence, and the law. Bias, confusion about instructions, or persuasive counsel can tilt the scales. That doesn't mean jurors are malicious. It means the system depends on imperfect people making hard calls.

Why do these myths stick? Partly because humans prefer tidy stories. It is easier to say someone is innocent than to sit with the uncertainty of evidence. Media narratives also simplify. A headline about an acquittal reads as a moral exclamation point. The truth is quieter, more complex, and less shareable.

Different Ways a Case Can End — Not All "Not Guilty" Are the Same

The public often lumps different court outcomes together. That clouds understanding.

Acquittal by jury is the classic image: twelve people return and say the defendant is not guilty. But cases also end in other ways that look similar at first glance:

- A judge can dismiss charges before trial if the evidence is insufficient or the prosecution committed serious errors.
- A case can be dropped by the prosecutor — sometimes because evidence is weak, sometimes because witnesses won't cooperate.
- There can be a hung jury: no one reaches a unanimous decision, and the judge declares a mistrial.
- Some systems have other verdicts — like "not proven" in Scotland — that communicate different legal meanings.

Each outcome carries different legal effects, and importantly, different emotional effects for the defendant, victim, and community. A dismissal might leave the defendant feeling relieved but bitter about the accusation. A jury acquittal might feel vindicating but still leave skepticism outside the courtroom.

The Legal Consequences People Misread

Many myths assume that criminal acquittal sweeps away all legal consequences. That's not true. Here are some realities that surprise people.

Civil Liability: The standard of proof in civil cases is lower — usually "preponderance of the evidence," meaning more likely than not. So someone acquitted criminally can still be liable in civil court for the same act. This difference doesn't offend logic; it derives from the idea that criminal punishment should only follow the most reliable findings because the stakes — liberty and stigma — are so high.

Double Jeopardy: In many countries, the constitution or law prevents the state from retrying someone after an acquittal for the same offense. In the United States, for example, the Fifth Amendment protects against double jeopardy (Source: U.S. Constitution, Fifth Amendment). But exceptions and technicalities exist, and other legal systems have different rules. When someone claims, "He can never be retried now," the safe answer is: in many places yes — but check the jurisdiction and the exact legal circumstances.

Administrative and Collateral Consequences: A criminal trial focuses on guilt or innocence in the narrow legal sense. But professional licensing bodies, employers, landlords, and immigration authorities are not bound by criminal verdicts in the same way. An acquittal might not undo a license suspension, an immigration proceeding, or an internal workplace investigation. Many jurisdictions have processes that allow a person to seek record sealing or expungement after an acquittal, but those processes are not automatic (Source: Legal Information Institute; state statutes differ).

Why Evidence Fails — It's Not Always Corruption

When evidence fails and someone is acquitted, people suspect corruption: bad cops, a weak prosecutor, a rigged jury. Sometimes those things happen. More commonly, the problem lies in human limits and legal rules.

Witness memory is fragile. Under stress, people make mistakes. Physical evidence can be contaminated or inconclusive. Investigators may follow a mistaken lead. Prosecutors, who must weigh every case against limited resources and political pressure, sometimes make strategic choices about what to charge. Defense lawyers, whose job is to create doubt, will point out every crack in the state's story. None of this proves a conspiracy; it shows the limits of human systems.

Here's another small scene: I spoke with a juror after a trial in which a local athlete was accused of assault. The juror told me she had been convinced by testimony at first, until a piece of video evidence showed a different angle. "I felt terrible," she said. "I wanted to get it right. I remember thinking: we're deciding a life." That quiet weight is what the system asks of jurors — and why reasonable doubt matters.

The Moral vs. The Legal

People struggle because law and morality are different languages. Law asks: did the prosecution prove its case under the rules it must follow? Morality asks: what is the right thing to believe or do? Those questions can point to different answers.

Imagine a person accused of a violent crime who admits responsibility to a friend but refuses to testify in court. The jurors don't hear the admission because it's excluded under hearsay rules. Legally, the state might fail to prove the case. Morally, some will feel the person is guilty. The law prefers a guy alone but given procedural fairness over a messy but possibly true confession that can't be verified or was obtained improperly.

That tension explains why acquittals sometimes feel like moral failures to the public. But the legal system was built on the idea that protecting procedural rights — even when it clouds the truth — is essential to preventing abuse.

Talking About an Acquittal Without Making Things Worse

When someone you know is acquitted, or when a case hits the news, what should you say? Here are the ideas I wish more people used.

Listen first. Let the people involved tell their story without judgment. Facts are often more complicated than headlines.

Avoid equating legal outcomes with moral worth. Saying "now they're innocent" or "they got away with it" shuts down conversation and deepens hurt.

Ask questions about what the verdict actually was. Did the case end in a jury acquittal? Was it dismissed? Was it a mistrial? Each has a different meaning and different consequences.

Recognize collateral harm. Even after an acquittal, people can be unemployed, scarred, or distrusted. A simple expression of empathy — "That must have been so hard" — goes farther than grand pronouncements.

If You're the One Acquitted: Practical Steps and Emotional Truths

If you are acquitted, the rush of relief can be immediate and then replaced — sometimes quickly — by a strange emptiness. Some people expect closure and find only more questions. If you walk out of court, here are some steps that help.

Talk to your lawyer about record options. In some places you can seek expungement or sealing of arrest records; in others, the process is more limited. A lawyer can explain the local rules.

Think about your public statement carefully. Saying too much can reopen wounds, but silence can be read as defiance. A short, honest note that thanks jurors and respects the process often works.

Seek support. Trials can be traumatic. Counseling, support groups, or simply friends who will listen quietly can make a big difference.

Accept that social consequences may take longer to heal than legal ones. People will form opinions. Rebuilding trust is a slow, patient process.

A Final Note on Fairness and Humility

Justice is messy because humans are messy. The legal system does not promise absolute truth; it promises a fair process with high protections against conviction. That design sometimes allows guilty people to walk free. It also prevents the state from wielding its vast power lightly. That trade-off is central to how liberal democracies think about punishment and liberty.

At the same time, we must be honest about the system's failings. Bias, unequal resources, and procedural glitches can create real injustice. Saying "not guilty" is not a magic eraser. It is a legal conclusion about a particular contest of proof on a particular day, given the evidence available and the rules that govern what evidence counts.

If you leave this chapter with one thing, let it be this: a not guilty verdict is a conclusion about the case the state presented, not a universal statement of moral truth. It invites us to be curious rather than certain, to ask how the evidence was gathered and what else might be true. It invites us to offer compassion — to the accused who has been through humiliation and the victim who may still carry pain.

The woman in the grocery line nodded when I explained that. She folded the idea inward, like a small careful secret. "So," she said, tapping her cart, "it's complicated." Yes, I told her. Most important things are. And the first step toward a fairer conversation about justice is to accept that complication — to speak about verdicts with *humility*, and to remember that justice is both a legal process and a human story.

Chapter 9

The Appeal Process After a Not Guilty Decision

The courtroom fell into a hush the moment the jury foreperson stood and read the words. He could feel his heart trying to climb out of his chest. Months of interviews, nights of notes, the way he'd rehearsed his explanations to strangers who didn't want to believe him — it all hung on those two syllables. *Not guilty.* For a while there was only the sound of people taking in a breath. Relief. Shock. Tears. And then, some weeks later, a letter arrived that changed the shape of relief into something more complicated: a notice that someone intended to challenge what the jury decided.

Most people think a not guilty verdict is an ending. That's the way it feels in the moment — a door swinging shut on fear. But the legal world is rarely this neat. Whether a verdict truly ends the story depends on where you are, who is appealing, and what the law allows. This chapter walks through that murky terrain: when an appeal after a not guilty decision makes sense, what steps an appeal follows, and what outcomes are possible — all told in a voice that tries to keep the law human-sized.

Why someone would appeal a not guilty verdict

A verdict is not an act of magic; it's the product of a long sequence of decisions made by judges, lawyers, witnesses, and jurors. Appeals are the mechanism the legal system uses to check those decisions. Still, not every unhappy person gets a do-over. In many places — including the United States — the government cannot retry someone after an acquittal because of *double jeopardy* protections (U.S. Constitution, Fifth Amendment). That means the space for appeals after a not guilty decision is narrow. But narrow does not mean empty.

There are a few distinct situations where a post-acquittal appeal might be possible or where other legal actions replace a traditional appeal. One is when the defendant, not the prosecution, seeks a legal ruling after trial — for example, to clear their record or to challenge an order that still casts a shadow over their life. Another is when the prosecution challenges pre-trial or interlocutory rulings that are not the verdict itself, such as a judge's decision to suppress evidence or to dismiss charges before a jury ever heard them. In some legal systems outside the U.S., the prosecution may be able to appeal an acquittal under limited circumstances. And sometimes what looks like an appeal is actually a collateral process: post-conviction motions, civil suits, or administrative hearings that address consequences of the trial rather than the underlying verdict.

The most common legal grounds for appealing — whether an appeal follows a guilty verdict or a quasi-appeal follows a not guilty one — fall into familiar categories. The claim that a court misunderstood the law. The argument that the judge made a procedural error so serious that it infected the fairness of the process. The accusation that jurors behaved improperly. Or the assertion that the entire trial was founded on evidence that should never have been admitted. Each of these ideas is simple in the abstract. In practice they are messy, textured, and fought over in pages of legal writing.

I remember a veteran public defender who once told me about a case where a client won an acquittal in state court only to find the district attorney quietly seeking permission to appeal a pretrial ruling about a search warrant. The defender described the feeling like being handed a clean shirt and being told to keep it clean until someone looks at it under ultraviolet light. It's a strange kind of vulnerability: you did everything right in the visible trial, but someone is asking a higher court to examine something that happened out of jury view. That scene captures why understanding grounds for appeal matters, even after a not guilty verdict.

Grounds for appealing a verdict — what courts will listen to

When people talk about grounds for appeal, they mean legal reasons a higher court should review or change what happened below. A few categories recur across most systems.

Errors of law. This is the classic. If the trial judge applied the wrong legal rule — for instance, instructing the jury in a way that misstated an element of the crime — an appellate court may be willing to step in. The question the higher court asks is usually whether applying the correct rule would have made any difference to the outcome.

Procedural mistakes. Courts rely on process to guarantee fairness. If a judge excluded the defendant's counsel at a crucial moment, allowed evidence that should have been kept out, or refused to allow a critical witness, those are procedural complaints. Appellate courts examine whether the error was significant enough to be called *prejudicial* — that is, whether it might have affected the verdict.

Juror misconduct. Jurors are supposed to decide the case based only on what they hear in court. If a juror speaks with a party, researches the case online, or brings outside information into deliberations, parties can ask for review. Proving misconduct is difficult; appellate courts are wary of second-guessing jury deliberations unless there is clear, credible evidence.

Insufficient evidence. This ground is tricky. A court reviewing a claim of insufficient evidence asks whether, looking at the evidence in the light most favorable to the verdict, a reasonable trier of fact could have found guilt beyond a reasonable doubt. After an acquittal, though, many systems will not allow the prosecution to challenge the jury's verdict on this basis because of double jeopardy protections.

Constitutional violations. Sometimes the issue is not a mistake in routine procedure but a breakdown in constitutional guarantees — for example, a coerced confession or a denial of effective assistance of counsel. These are serious claims, and appellate courts take them seriously because they touch on the fairness of the entire justice system.

The thread that runs through these grounds is that appellate courts are not re-trying the case. They are asking whether legal rules were followed, whether safeguards held, and whether the process protected the parties' rights. That focus — law over fact-finding — is crucial and shapes how appeals are argued and decided.

How the appellate process unfolds

An appeal is a kind of legal choreography. It moves through predictable stages, but the rhythm and timing differ depending on the court, the jurisdiction, and the posture of the case.

The first step is notice. If a party intends to seek review, they usually must file a notice of appeal within a short window after the final judgment. In many systems this is counted in days or weeks. Miss the deadline and the appellate gate closes. That early deadline creates pressure and forces quick decisions about which grounds to pursue.

Next comes the record on appeal. The record is the trial transcript, exhibits, and all filings that show what happened below. The appellant asks the higher court to review that record. Appellate judges do not typically admit new evidence. The appeal is based on the paperwork and testimony already on file.

Briefing follows. The appellant writes a legal brief explaining the errors they claim, the relevant law, and the remedy they seek. The appellee — the party who won below — files an answering brief defending the verdict. These documents are dense with citations, but their purpose is simple: persuade judges that the lower court was right or wrong on particular legal questions.

Many appeals include oral argument, though not all. In oral argument, lawyers have a limited time to make their case to the panel of appellate judges. This is the moment that can feel theatrical: a judge interrupts, a lawyer defends a turn of phrase, and new angles sometimes emerge. But the live exchange is only part of the process; judges have the briefs, the record, and their own notes to guide their decision.

Then comes the opinion. Appellate courts may affirm the lower court, reverse it, or reverse in part and remand the case for further proceedings. Opinions explain the judges' reasoning. These written decisions are the lifeblood of common law systems because they guide future cases.

There are possible further stages: requests for rehearing, appeals to a higher appellate court, or petitions for review by a supreme court. These steps are discretionary. Higher courts take only a fraction of requests, choosing those that raise important legal questions or correct conflicting lower court rulings.

Throughout this process, two realities shape strategy. One is the standard of review: appellate courts give different levels of deference depending on whether the issue is factual or legal. Legal questions are reviewed *de novo* — with fresh eyes. Factual findings get more respect and are usually overturned only if clearly erroneous. The second reality is preservation: you generally cannot raise an issue on appeal that you did not object to in the trial court. That rule punishes strategizing after the fact and forces immediate, on-the-record objections.

The special case of appeals after an acquittal

Because an acquittal is often the last word in criminal guilt, the usual appellate playbook changes. Prosecutors cannot, as a rule, retry a defendant after an acquittal. That is the double jeopardy rule. But appellate activity can still occur around the edges.

Sometimes the appeal is not an appeal from the verdict but from a prior decision unconnected to the jury's choice. A prosecutor might appeal an order that dismissed some charges before trial or suppressed key evidence. In other cases, the government might seek appellate review of a procedural ruling when that ruling is separable from the verdict and hasn't yet triggered double jeopardy protections.

Another path is collateral attack. Even if a direct appeal is unavailable, parties may bring separate motions or suits that challenge legal aspects of the case that survived the trial. A defendant acquitted of criminal charges might still face civil liability or administrative consequences (professional licensing, immigration issues). Those arenas have their own appeal routes.

What can happen — possible outcomes and their consequences

An appellate court's decision is rarely a yes-or-no switch. The range of possible outcomes reflects the different mistakes the court might find and how it decides to fix them.

Affirmation is the simplest result. The appellate court finds no reversible error and leaves the verdict intact. For a defendant, affirmation of a not guilty verdict means the legal path has mostly closed — barring extraordinary petitions.

Reversal and remand is the more dramatic result. If an appellate court finds a legal error that undermined the trial's fairness, it may reverse the judgment and send the case back to the trial court with instructions. Sometimes the court directs that a new trial be held. But here is where double jeopardy re-enters: in many jurisdictions, retrial after reversal of an acquittal is barred. In other situations, especially where the error relates to pretrial rulings or procedural missteps, a retrial may be permitted.

Partial reversal is common. The appellate court might find some errors but not all, or it might vacate certain convictions or offenses while leaving others in place. In civil cases, appellate courts can remand for recalculation of damages while affirming liability findings.

Dismissal is a possible remedy when the appellate court decides the procedural defects are so severe that the only fair outcome is to dismiss charges. That outcome is rare but powerful.

Then there are post-appellate consequences outside the criminal record. Even after a not guilty verdict survives review, collateral matters may linger. Civil suits, administrative actions, professional discipline, and immigration processes can proceed on different tracks. Sometimes expungement or sealing of records is available; other times the acquittal does not automatically erase the legal scrawl left on official files.

Why the appeals process feels so personal

Legal rules are formal and impersonal, but appeals touch people at an intimate level. I think of the parent who sits in the back of a courtroom after an acquittal and watches the defendant rebuild a life. The sense of relief turns careful; they worry that a victory on paper might not translate to a clean break from suspicion. Or the prosecutor who, convinced of the strength of their case, faces an appellate loss and must reconcile public scrutiny with professional humility. The law asks communities to live with outcomes that are sometimes messy and to balance finality with fairness.

That human tension explains why strategy matters. Defense lawyers often make different choices when they anticipate post-trial challenge: preserve issues on the record, insist on careful jury instructions, and keep an eye on collateral proceedings. Prosecutors, too, must weigh whether seeking review will do more harm than good — both for a public office and for the people involved.

Practical steps for people affected by post-verdict appeals

If you find yourself on the receiving end of an appeal after a not guilty decision — whether you are the defendant, a victim, or a family member — a few practical rules help steady the ground. First, understand the distinction between direct appeals and collateral challenges. Second, don't assume the finality of a verdict without checking the local rules on double jeopardy and interlocutory appeals. Third, consult counsel early. Appeals are time-sensitive, and missing a filing deadline can forfeit rights. Finally, pay attention to collateral risks: civil filings, administrative proceedings, and public records can shape a life long after a verdict.

A small resolution and a big point

The truth about appeals after a not guilty verdict is that they are both rarer and more complicated than a news headline suggests. Many acquittals are indeed final, and many appeals never succeed. Yet the possibility of challenge shapes how trials are run, how lawyers prepare, and how families process the outcome. That reality asks something of everyone involved: patience, clarity about legal boundaries, and an acceptance that finality in law is a cautious promise rather than an absolute one.

If you take anything from this chapter, let it be this: a not guilty verdict is powerful, but understanding the legal landscape around it — the limited grounds for appeal, the steps the process follows, and the range of potential outcomes — gives you the best chance of protecting whatever freedom or peace that verdict created. Talk to an attorney who knows the rules where you are. Preserve the record. And if you're the one sitting with relief after a verdict, watch the quiet months that follow with a sober eye. The law has its rituals for review; your future depends on knowing which ones apply.

Chapter 10

Legal Rights After a Not Guilty Verdict

The judge says the words you have been waiting for: *not guilty*. For a moment the courtroom seems to tilt back into the familiar world — the hum of fluorescent lights, the squeak of polished shoes. You breathe. You cry. You call someone who answers on the first ring. Relief pours in like warm water.

Then the relief thins. You remember the news article that named you. You remember a background check that stopped a job offer. You remember the whispered question in the grocery line. A not guilty verdict clears the criminal charge, but it does not erase everything that happened, nor does it always end the legal stories still attached to your life. There are rights, limits, and options — but they are layered and uneven. This chapter walks through the three things people ask about most after an acquittal: privacy and record sealing; limits on retrial or further prosecution; and the opportunities, if any, for civil claims or compensation.

I once sat with a woman named Maya in a small café after her acquittal. She laughed at the absurdity of the headlines and then cried when she showed me a screenshot: her case, the arrest photo, the prosecutor's statement, all still live on a local news site. "They called me a suspect in the headline for months," she said. "The judge cleared me, but the article is still there like a scar." Her story is not unusual. For people who are found not guilty, the legal victory can feel both complete and incomplete — a mix of exoneration and lingering public record.

Privacy and Record Sealing: What an Acquittal Can and Can't Quiet

After a not guilty verdict, many people want the same thing: to close the door on the case. They imagine a sealed folder and a clear background check. In some places and in some cases, that is possible. In many others, the reality is messier.

A criminal *acquittal* is different from a *dismissal* or *expungement*. An acquittal means the state failed to prove guilt beyond a reasonable doubt. It does not always change the status of official records created when you were arrested, charged, or tried. Arrest records, police reports, charging documents, and court dockets can remain public, searchable, and persistent online long after the verdict.

Sealing and expungement are legal tools that can limit public access to those records. The specifics depend heavily on where you are. Some states offer automatic sealing in certain cases after an acquittal; others require you to file a petition and meet specific criteria. Federal cases are a different animal; sealing federal records is more complicated and often requires a higher showing of need.

When you ask a lawyer about sealing, they'll ask where the case was tried and what the charge was. Laws vary in how they treat acquittals. Some jurisdictions make a clear distinction: acquittal equals a stronger claim for sealing. Others treat acquittals more like dismissals, with similar procedural hurdles. For example, a state might allow sealing if the prosecution doesn't refile charges within a certain time, while another might require a judge to find that public interest in the record's availability is outweighed by your privacy interest.

Beyond the courthouse, there is the internet. News outlets and social media platforms keep content alive. A sealed court file won't automatically erase an article or a cached search result. Companies that sell arrest records and background checks operate in a space that doesn't always respond to court orders in the same way. You might have to use a mix of legal petitions and private reputation services — or simply ask news outlets to update or remove old pieces. Some outlets will, especially after an acquittal; others will not.

One quiet truth is that sealing helps with formal checks: employment background screenings, licensing boards, and government record searches. It can make it legally permissible to say you have no conviction and reduce the number of stumbling blocks when applying for jobs, housing, or professional licenses. But sealing is rarely a magic eraser. For many people, it is the first step — an important one — toward restoring privacy and rebuilding a life.

(Source: Innocence Project; National Conference of State Legislatures)

Practical steps after an acquittal for privacy

- Start by getting certified court records of the outcome. A judge's verdict or clerk's certificate is the primary document you will use in petitions.
- Consult a lawyer about sealing or expungement in the jurisdiction where you were arrested and tried. Procedures and eligibility differ by state and federal court.
- Request removal or correction from consumer reporting companies and background-check firms. They may require documentation of the acquittal or a sealing order.
- Contact news outlets with a calm, factual request to correct or update articles. Some will add editors' notes after an acquittal.
- Consider reputation-management services as a last resort. They can be costly and do not guarantee removal, but they can help dilute harmful search results.

Limitations on Retrial or Prosecution: The Promise and the Limits of Double Jeopardy

"Once you beat it, you beat it for good," is a comforting line many people hear. The principle behind that comfort is the Double Jeopardy Clause of the Fifth Amendment to the U.S. Constitution, which says that no person shall "be subject for the same offense to be twice put in jeopardy of life or limb." In short, you cannot be tried twice by the same sovereign for the same offense after an acquittal.

That promise matters. It protects against the state's power to grind on someone through repeated trials until it wins. It means a jury's verdict of not guilty should, in principle, be the end of the criminal case at that level.

But constitutional law is not poetry; it's full of exceptions, doctrines, and limitations. One of the most important is the *dual-sovereignty doctrine*: the federal government and a state government are separate sovereigns. That means a person acquitted in state court can, in some circumstances, be tried in federal court for the same fundamental conduct if the federal government has a different sovereign interest and the conduct violated federal law as well. The U.S. Supreme Court reaffirmed that doctrine in Gamble v. United States (2019). The practical upshot: an acquittal at the state level is not always a universal shield.

There are also tactical and procedural complexities. A retrial in the same court after a guilty verdict is barred by double jeopardy, but a mistrial or certain kinds of appeals can reopen territory. Prosecutors sometimes try to bring different charges based on the same facts; whether that triggers double jeopardy depends on whether the charges are considered the same "offense" under legal tests that courts use. The "same-elements" test — whether each statutory element of the later offense is also an element of the earlier offense — is one common analysis.

There are other ways cases can return. If new, admissible evidence emerges — especially if it shows perjury or fraud at trial — prosecutors might pursue different legal theories. And in rare and extreme cases, federal involvement, separate jurisdictions, or conduct that crosses state lines can mean a different prosecutor can pick up the baton.

This reality is an uncomfortable one for many who believed acquittal equals finality. It is also a reason defendants often ask for more: not just a verdict of not guilty, but plea bargains that include dismissal language or official letters from prosecutors noting the case is closed. Those documents can sometimes be persuasive to other agencies or media outlets.

(Source: U.S. Constitution, Fifth Amendment; Gamble v. United States, 587 U.S. ___ (2019))

How to protect against surprise prosecutions

There is no single bulletproof move, but a few actions help reduce your risk:

- Keep documentation of the not guilty verdict — certified copies of the judgment and clerk's minutes.
- Ask your lawyer for a written statement from the prosecutor's office confirming no further charges are pending, if possible.

- If the conduct might attract federal interest (for example, crossing state lines, fraud that targets federal programs), consult an attorney who understands federal criminal statutes.
- Be cautious about public statements that could be misread or used in other jurisdictions. Silence sometimes preserves legal space.

Opportunities for Civil Action or Compensation: Seeking Redress After Wrongful Harm

The criminal system and the civil system are different roads. A not guilty verdict in criminal court doesn't automatically create a path to compensation. But sometimes it opens doors — or at least standing — for civil actions.

There are a few routes people pursue after being acquitted: civil suits for malicious prosecution, false arrest or imprisonment, defamation claims, and statutory compensation programs for wrongful convictions or prosecutions. Each has its own threshold.

Malicious prosecution claims are about the abuse of the criminal process. To win a malicious prosecution case, most courts require proof that the prior criminal proceedings ended in the plaintiff's favor (an acquittal usually suffices), that the defendant initiated or continued the prosecution without probable cause, and that it was done with malice or improper purpose. Winning such a case is not easy. Prosecutors enjoy broad immunity for their official actions in many contexts, and police officers have qualified immunity for many actions unless they violated clearly established rights. The standards for police civil liability were clarified and tightened in a number of Supreme Court cases, meaning those suits face significant hurdles.

False arrest or false imprisonment suits focus more narrowly on whether law enforcement had legal authority to detain or arrest. If an officer lacked probable cause for an arrest and you were detained, you may have a stronger claim than in malicious prosecution contexts because the initial threshold is lower — did the officer have a reasonable basis to arrest you? But even here, courts look at what the officer believed at the time and whether that belief was reasonable.

Defamation claims — libel and slander — address false statements made to a third party that harm reputation. Media outlets have significant protections for reporting on public records and events, and the standard is higher if the subject is a public figure. For private individuals, successful defamation suits still require proving falsity, harm, and sometimes negligence. After an acquittal, an outright claim that a news outlet called you a criminal when a judge found you not guilty can sometimes succeed where the underlying news coverage misstated facts or relied on falsehoods.

Separate from civil suits are statutory compensation programs. Some states have laws that provide financial compensation to people who were wrongfully convicted and later exonerated. These bills often come after long advocacy by innocence organizations and exonerees. Eligibility rules vary — some programs require a certificate of wrongful conviction from a governor or a court, some require a finding of actual innocence, and others exclude cases where the convicted person pleaded guilty even if they later recanted. The amounts also vary wildly by state.

What about a person who was acquitted rather than convicted? Compensation statutes typically target wrongful convictions, and an acquittal is not the same as a declaration of innocence. That does not mean there are no paths to recovery after an acquittal, but it makes the road narrower. If you suffered clear constitutional violations — for example, illegal searches, coerced confessions, or civil rights violations — you might have a civil rights claim under federal law (Section 1983) or under state tort law. These claims can be powerful but are often complex and expensive to pursue.

(Source: Innocence Project; various state statutes on wrongful conviction compensation)

Choosing a path: practical considerations when thinking about civil options

You should balance legal strategy with practical realities. Civil suits are expensive, time-consuming, and emotionally draining. Even if you win, collecting money is not always easy, especially against government defendants who may have immunities or limited indemnity. Consider these factors:

- Liability: who is the defendant? Police? Prosecutors? Media outlets? Private individuals?
- Immunity: prosecutors often have absolute immunity for charging decisions; law enforcement enjoys qualified immunity in many contexts.

- Evidence: can you show malice, lack of probable cause, or actual falsity?

- Costs and timing: civil cases can take years and require depositions, expert witnesses, and discovery.

- Non-monetary goals: sometimes the aim is an apology, correction, or public vindication rather than compensation. A carefully crafted letter, settlement negotiations, or public records requests can sometimes achieve that without a full lawsuit.

An anecdote about choosing justice

I remember a man named Daniel — not his real name — who was acquitted after an ugly public investigation. He wanted money, and not just for bills but for the principle of it: the job he lost, the portrait in his children's minds, the mortgage he almost lost. He spoke to three lawyers. One offered a high-energy advertising video promising millions. Another described the legal hurdles and the long odds. The third listened and said, "If you want money, we evaluate the likely defendants and their immunity. If you want the record cleared and your name restored locally, we start with the newspaper editors." They chose the third path first. They negotiated corrections with the news outlet, which published a modest but sincere editor's note. It didn't solve everything, but it stopped the bleeding. Later, a targeted civil suit for false imprisonment — where the facts strongly supported lack of probable cause — produced a modest settlement that covered legal fees and paid for counseling for his children. He told me he felt, finally, like he had regained a thread of normalcy.

After the verdict: a checklist toward restoration

You don't have to wait to feel better; there are concrete things you can do to rebuild:

- Gather your documents: certified judgment, arrest records, bail paperwork, police reports, transcripts.

- Speak with an attorney who specializes in post-conviction remedies or civil rights. Ask about sealing, expungement, civil suits, and statutory compensation.

- Reach out to advocacy groups: innocence projects, legal aid clinics, and local bar associations often offer free advice or referrals.

- Preserve evidence: save emails, screenshots, recordings, and dates of lost opportunities like job denials.

- Manage online reputation: request corrections from news sites, dispute inaccurate background reports, and consider professional help if needed.

- Tell your story on your terms to trusted people — not to derail legal strategies but to reclaim the narrative from rumors and headlines.

The emotional thread: beyond law to life

Laws and forms matter. They make possible the quiet restoration of privacy and sometimes the relief of money. But an acquittal also leaves emotional work. People return to jobs or find the job is gone. Relationships strained by an investigation don't fix themselves. Children may have witnessed the fear. Even after courts say not guilty, community trust may need time to rebuild.

That is part of why many people look for non-legal answers alongside legal ones: therapy, support groups, trusted community leaders, and time. One woman I met after her acquittal started volunteering at a neighborhood clinic. She said showing up and serving people who had nothing to do with her case soothed something that law could not: the social heartbeat that says you belong.

A closing thought — what you can ask for, and what you can expect

A not guilty verdict is powerful. It is a formal rejection of guilt by the criminal justice system. But the verdict is the beginning of a different kind of work: sealing records when possible, understanding the limits of double jeopardy and separate sovereigns, and evaluating civil or statutory routes for recovery if you have been harmed.

If you or someone you love has been acquitted, start with documentation and trusted legal counsel. Know that the law offers protections and remedies, but also that the path forward will likely blend legal strategy with practical and emotional rebuilding. Seek support, prioritize mental health, and be patient. The world may take time to catch up with the verdict. You can — through deliberate, sometimes small steps — help make it catch up sooner.

If you want, I can help outline the likely process in your state, suggest questions to ask a lawyer, or draft a letter asking a news outlet to correct an article after an acquittal. The law shapes what is possible; community shapes what is healed. Between them lies the work of reclaiming a life.

Chapter 11

Responsibilities in defending clients effectively

You are the person who stands up for someone who is facing charges. The core of being an effective defender is to help your client navigate the legal process while staying within the rules and keeping things fair for everyone involved. This means balancing a fierce commitment to your client's interests with a clear respect for the law and for justice itself.

Step 1: Understand the client's goals and rights. Begin by listening carefully to what your client wants to achieve. Explain, in plain language, what is realistically possible given the facts and the law. Your job is to help your client make informed choices, not to promise a guaranteed outcome. This clarity protects both of you: it sets realistic expectations and helps you design a plan that fits the client's needs and the truth of the case.

Step 2: Build a solid, ethical defense. Review every piece of evidence, look for weaknesses, and identify the best strategies that stay within the rules. A strong defense asks hard questions: Is any key evidence improperly obtained? Are there procedures that were not followed? Could there be an alternate explanation for what happened? Your aim is to uncover the truth as it relates to the case and to present a clear, evidence-based argument to the court.

Step 3: Communicate honestly and with respect. Keep your client informed about progress, risks, and possible results. Explain decisions in a way they can understand, and obtain their informed consent before moving forward with a particular strategy. In court, present information truthfully and avoid overstating what you can prove. Honesty builds trust with your client and with the court, and it protects both of you from later problems.

Step 4: Maintain professional competence and fairness. Stay up to date with general defense practice and ethical norms. Seek guidance from colleagues when faced with unfamiliar issues, and always consider whether actions respect the rights of others involved, including victims and witnesses. A defender who acts with integrity helps preserve the dignity of the legal process.

Example: A client is charged with shoplifting. You carefully review the store's surveillance footage and interview witnesses. You discuss two potential defenses: one could be that the client did not intend to steal, and another could be an issue with how the evidence was collected. You explain these options, highlight risks, and help the client decide which path to take. Regardless of the path chosen, you document every decision and proceed honestly through every step of the case.

Keeping this balance—zealous representation without bending the rules—safeguards your client and upholds the system's trust. It also teaches younger readers that defending someone is not about winning at any cost; it's about pursuing truth, fairness, and the right outcomes within the law.

Managing client confidentiality and honesty

Confidentiality is a cornerstone of the attorney-client relationship. It means what you discuss with your client stays private, with only a few very specific exceptions. This protection encourages clients to share all the facts, even information that might seem embarrassing or harmful. When you respect confidentiality, you gain a clearer picture of the case and a stronger foundation for a fair defense.

Step 1: Define what counts as confidential. Explain to your client that most conversations, notes, and documents shared with you remain private. Clarify any limits: for example, certain information might need to be disclosed if there is a risk of serious harm or as required by court rules. Clear boundaries help prevent accidental leaks and protect trust.

Step 2: Keep records secure. Store notes, emails, and files in a safe, organized way. Use systems that limit who can access sensitive information. Good organization makes it easier to prepare a defense and to respect privacy.

Step 3: Balance honesty with confidentiality. There will be times you must tell the court or investigators things that affect the case. You do this carefully, ensuring you do not reveal more than is necessary and always staying truthful about the facts. If something could be misinterpreted, you explain it clearly rather than leaving room for doubt.

Step 4: Guard against conflicts of interest. If you represent more than one client who could be adverse to each other, or if new information creates a potential conflict, you must handle it openly. That could mean disclosing the conflict to your client or, when needed, stepping aside from the case. Protecting confidentiality also means protecting the client's right to a fair, impartial defense.

Example: A defense attorney learns a client lied about a key detail early in the case. The attorney explains the issue to the client and discusses how it affects the defense plan. The client decides to disclose the truth in a controlled, appropriate way. The attorney then helps ensure the disclosure is handled in a way that preserves confidentiality for other parts of the case while meeting ethical duties to the court.

Honesty within confidentiality is not about hiding inconvenient truths; it's about sharing what is necessary to pursue a just result while honoring the trust placed in you. When you uphold these standards, you model responsible conduct for younger readers who may someday stand in a courtroom themselves.

Strategies to uphold justice and integrity

Upholding justice and integrity means making choices that keep the process fair, transparent, and respectful for everyone involved. You defend not just a client, but the idea that laws govern society and apply equally to all.

Step 1: Avoid overpromising outcomes. You cannot guarantee how a case will end. Being honest about uncertainties helps manage expectations and maintain credibility with your client and the court. It also teaches readers that responsible defense relies on careful analysis, not bravado.

Step 2: Present evidence ethically. Do not mislead or manipulate facts. Explain evidence accurately, highlight its strengths and weaknesses, and advocate for the most persuasive interpretation within the law. This approach strengthens the case's integrity and helps the truth emerge.

Step 3: Respect the rights of others involved. Treat witnesses, victims, and prosecutors with civility. A respectful posture invites fair testimony and reduces unnecessary confrontation. It shows that you care about the process as a whole, not just the client's outcome.

Step 4: Seek fairness above victory. When you identify errors in the process—procedural missteps, misapplied rules, or biased procedures—raise them politely and clearly. Correcting mistakes protects the integrity of the system and helps prevent injustice, even if it costs your client a quick win.

Example: During a hearing, you notice a procedural issue that could affect the outcome. You raise the issue with the judge, present the relevant facts, and propose a legitimate remedy that stays within the rules. The result may be a longer process, but it strengthens the case's fairness and reliability.

Troubleshooting

1) Problem: A client pressures you to hide information or mislead the court. Fix: Explain the limits of confidentiality and the obligation to be truthful; document decisions and explore legal avenues to address concerns without compromising ethics.

2) Problem: A potential conflict of interest arises. Fix: Disclose promptly, assess whether you can continue to represent the client fairly, and consider stepping aside if needed to protect the client's rights and the process.

3) Problem: You face a highly emotional or aggressive client. Fix: Set clear boundaries, communicate calmly, and keep the focus on lawful, ethical strategies that serve long-term justice.

4) Problem: You discover information that could harm your client's case if revealed. Fix: Seek guidance on how to handle it legally and ethically, and discuss options with the client to determine the best course within the rules.

Resources

Templates and tools can help you stay ethical and organized. Consider using:

- Client intake and goal-setting template, to capture goals, risks, and consent.
- Confidentiality agreement outline, to define what stays private and what may be disclosed.
- Conflict-of-interest disclosure checklist, to detect and document potential issues early.

- Case notes and evidence checklist, to keep track of what has been reviewed and what remains.

End transition

In the next chapter, you will explore Protecting Your Rights During Trials: Knowing your legal rights as a defendant, the importance of legal representation, and tips for effective courtroom behavior. This chapter builds on the ethical foundations you've examined here, showing how ethical practice supports fair and strong advocacy when you step into a courtroom.

Chapter 12

Knowing your legal rights as a defendant

When you are facing a criminal case, your rights are your protections. Knowing them helps you navigate the process without unintentionally giving up important safeguards. In many places, you have the right to know why you are being charged, to have a lawyer, to a fair and public trial, and to present your side of the story.

Key rights you should know include:

- The right to be told what you are accused of. You deserve clear information about the charges, the evidence, and the court dates.

- The right to a lawyer. If you cannot afford one, in many places a public defender or court-appointed attorney can help. A lawyer can explain complicated words, help you understand options, and protect your rights.

- The right to remain silent. You do not have to answer questions that might incriminate you. You can choose to speak with your attorney present, and your attorney can help decide what, if anything, you should say.

- The right to a fair trial. This includes the right to hear the evidence against you, to question witnesses, and to present your own witnesses or evidence.

- The right to be treated with respect and dignity. Courts should be organized so you are not rushed or forced to make quick decisions you don't understand.

- The right to a timely process. Trials should move forward without unnecessary delays, so you don't have to wait months or years.

Practical tips to protect these rights:

- Ask for a lawyer as soon as you are brought to a serious questioning or charged with a crime. If you're unsure, say you want to speak with a lawyer before answering questions.

- Do not sign documents or admit guilt without your lawyer's advice. Written statements can be used later, so read carefully and think before you sign.

- Keep track of dates, names, and what happened. Simple notes can help you and your lawyer build a clearer picture.

- If you feel unsure about something the judge or police say, ask your lawyer to explain. You do not have to understand everything immediately—your lawyer can translate legal language into plain terms.

Examples in everyday life:

- A student on trial for a school incident would still have basic rights, including the right to know what they are accused of and the right to talk with a lawyer before answering questions about the incident.

- In any case, you can request time to discuss with your attorney before making statements or decisions, so you do not feel pressured into a rushed choice.

Remember, exercising your rights is not about being difficult. It is about making sure you are treated fairly and that the people deciding your case understand your side clearly. Rights are the tools you use to level the playing field when you are under pressure.

Importance of legal representation

A lawyer is your guide through the courtroom. They know the rules, what kinds of evidence are allowed, and how trials are structured. Having a lawyer helps you understand the charges, judge the strength of the other side's case, and plan a strategy that fits your situation.

Reasons to have strong legal representation:

- They explain complex rules. The law is full of rules about what evidence can be used, how witnesses are questioned, and what must be proven for a conviction. A lawyer translates and applies these rules to your case.

- They protect your rights during questioning. They can object to improper questions, insist on having a lawyer present, and prevent you from saying something that could hurt your case.

- They manage paperwork and deadlines. Court dates, forms, and notices pile up quickly. A lawyer keeps track so nothing slips through the cracks.

- They prepare a clear defense. Your lawyer gathers evidence, contacts witnesses, and helps you decide which arguments to use. They can suggest strategies you might not have thought of on your own.

- They negotiate. In some cases, lawyers discuss possible plea agreements or reduced charges. A careful negotiation can avoid a worse outcome than going to trial.

Two simple examples show how representation helps:

- Example 1: You are accused of a mistake at a neighborhood event. Your lawyer reviews the evidence and discovers a missing logbook that shows you were elsewhere at the time. This weakens the link between you and the alleged event and supports an alternative explanation.

- Example 2: During a trial, the other side introduces a piece of evidence that was collected improperly. Your lawyer files a motion to exclude that evidence, which can change the strength of the case against you. Even the possibility of excluding questionable evidence can change the strategy of the entire defense.

What to look for in a good lawyer:

- Experience with your type of case. A lawyer who understands the specific rules and common defenses in your jurisdiction is valuable.

- Clear communication. You should feel heard and understand the plan. If you feel confused, ask for simpler explanations.

- Accessibility and responsiveness. You want someone who returns calls or messages in a reasonable time and keeps you informed of any developments.

- A respectful approach. You deserve to be treated with courtesy, honesty, and patience, even when the information is tough to hear.

If you cannot afford private legal help, remember that many places offer publicly funded defense services or court-appointed attorneys. It is okay to ask about these options early in the process so you can secure the support you need to present your side well.

Tips for effective courtroom behavior

Your conduct in the courtroom matters as much as the facts of the case. Calm, respectful, and clear behavior helps the judge and jury focus on your story and the evidence in the record.

Guidelines to follow:

- Address the judge properly. Use "Your Honor" when speaking to the judge, and wait for cues before speaking.

- Listen carefully and speak clearly. Before you answer, take a breath, think about your words, and speak in simple sentences.

- Do not interrupt others. Let prosecutors, witnesses, and your attorney finish their points before you respond.

- Follow your attorney's lead. Your lawyer will tell you when to speak, what to say, and when to stay silent. Trust that guidance.

- Be honest, but concise. Answer only what is asked, and avoid volunteering details that do not help your defense.

- Keep your body calm. Sit still, avoid fidgeting, and maintain a respectful posture. If you feel overwhelmed, signal your attorney to request a short break.

- Dress appropriately. Clean, simple clothing shows respect for the process and helps you feel more focused.

- Do not discuss the case outside the courtroom. Information shared with family or friends can confuse your defense or be used against you.

- Respect privacy. Don't try to influence witnesses, and avoid sharing private information about others involved in the case.

Concrete examples of courtroom behavior:

- During a hearing, you pause after the judge asks a question, take a breath, and answer clearly, using short sentences like, "Yes, Your Honor" or "No, Your Honor," followed by a brief explanation when requested.
- If a cross-examination asks about a sensitive detail, your lawyer may object if the question is beyond the scope of the case or could unfairly pressure you. You remain calm, and your lawyer handles the rest.
- If you need a moment to think, you can say, "Your Honor, I need a moment to think about that," and the judge usually grants a brief pause. Your attorney uses that time to guide your response.

Common courtroom pitfalls and quick fixes:

- Pitfall: Answering questions without thinking. Fix: Pause, ask for a moment to think, and confer with your lawyer if needed.
- Pitfall: Showing anger or sarcasm toward witnesses or the court. Fix: Breathe, stay respectful, and focus on delivering a clear answer.
- Pitfall: Signaling guilt by over-sharing. Fix: Let your attorney present your side; avoid guessing or admitting things you're unsure about.
- Pitfall: Ignoring the dress or behavior norms. Fix: Dress neatly, be punctual, and show readiness to participate.

Checklists you can use before a session or hearing:

- Have I spoken with my lawyer and understood the plan for this session?
- Do I know the question I'm about to answer, and have I prepared a concise, truthful response?
- Am I dressed and behaving with respect for the court and others?
- Do I have any documents or notes that are allowed to be shown, and have I reviewed them with my lawyer?
- Am I ready to wait calmly if the judge or prosecutor asks for a pause?

The aim is not to pretend to be perfect, but to be prepared, honest, and composed. When you act with care, you help the process see your side more clearly and you protect your rights at the same time.

In the next chapter, you will explore how the jury and the judge make decisions in Not Guilty outcomes. You will learn about the jury deliberation process and the standards of proof they use, how a judge gives instructions and their impact on verdicts, and the ongoing effort to keep trials fair for everyone involved. Specifically, you'll examine:

1) Jury deliberation process and standards of proof,
2) Judge's instructions and impact on verdicts,
3) Ensuring fairness in trial proceedings.

Chapter 13

You will learn how juries deliberate, how judges give instructions, and how trials stay fair, so not guilty outcomes come from careful, evidence-based reasoning.

Jury Deliberation Process and Standards of Proof

Juries are the group of everyday people chosen to weigh evidence in a criminal case. After all the witnesses have spoken and the lawyers have finished their closing arguments, jurors step into a private room to begin deliberations. They read through the evidence again, discuss how strongly each piece supports or weakens guilt, and listen to one another's ideas. They talk until they reach a verdict, or until the group decides they cannot agree. In criminal cases, the standard is "beyond a reasonable doubt." That phrase means a juror must be firmly convinced of guilt based on the facts and the law. If a juror has a reasonable doubt about guilt, that doubt should prevent a guilty verdict.

Deliberation is not a single moment of certainty. It is a careful conversation where jurors compare notes, test interpretations, and check whether their feelings fit with the evidence presented in court. Sometimes a juror feels sure about a fingerprint or a piece of video, while another juror needs more time to examine whether that piece really connects to the crime. In such moments, jurors may ask to re-examine exhibits, review witness testimony, or read instructions again to ground their conclusions in the facts. The aim is fairness, not speed; a true not guilty verdict should reflect a careful weighing of all available information.

Two short, practical examples help show how this works in practice. Example 1: In a hypothetical case about a bicycle theft, fingerprints are found on a chair near where the bike was kept. Some jurors see the print as a clear link to the suspect, while others worry about how the print got there. They discuss alternative explanations and review the chain of custody for the evidence. After thoughtful discussion, they decide that the fingerprints do not definitively prove who took the bike, so guilt is not established beyond a reasonable doubt. Example 2: In another hypothetical scenario, jurors strongly disagree about whether a late-night text message proves a person's intent. They request more time and ask the judge to review the concept of intent in light of the law and the surrounding circumstances. Through careful debate, they reach a verdict that reflects the balance of evidence and the standard of proof.

A key idea here is that the prosecution must prove guilt beyond a reasonable doubt, and the defense can challenge that proof. Jurors are allowed to rely on reasonable inferences—logical conclusions drawn from the facts presented—but they should not base a verdict on guesswork, stereotypes, or outside rumors. The goal of deliberation is to reach a verdict that follows the evidence and the law, not to find a winner or punish someone unfairly. If the group cannot agree after a thorough discussion, some jurisdictions permit a hung jury, which may lead to a new trial or an approved conclusion that the case ends without a verdict on guilt. In every case, fairness rides on the jurors' willingness to examine the evidence honestly and to listen to each other with respect.

Judge's Instructions and Impact on Verdicts

Before deliberations begin, the judge delivers official instructions. These are like a map showing jurors how to move through the case step by step. The judge explains what kinds of evidence count, how to judge the credibility of witnesses, and what the law says about the burden of proof. A clear instruction helps jurors understand what to consider and what to ignore, and it sets the rules for how to measure guilt or innocence.

The impact of these instructions on verdicts is powerful. Clear explanations of "beyond a reasonable doubt" help prevent jurors from thinking guilt must be proven with certainty or beyond any doubt, which would be impossible in most real-world cases. Instructions about how to evaluate credibility can prevent overreliance on a single witness or a dramatic moment on the stand. Instructions that remind jurors to consider only properly admitted evidence help them avoid letting in things the judge has ruled out as unreliable. When instructions are precise and comprehensible, jurors are more likely to apply the law correctly and to reach a verdict that matches the evidence.

Two scenarios show how judge's instructions shape outcomes. Scenario A: The judge explicitly explains that a single eye-witness account can be enough to establish guilt beyond a reasonable doubt if the account is credible and corroborated by other evidence. Jurors then weigh that testimony with other facts and discuss whether the evidence as a whole meets the standard. Scenario B: The judge takes care to remind jurors that they must not consider information that was not entered into evidence or that the lawyers argued about but the court did not admit. This prevents jurors from being swayed by rumors or emotional appeals and keeps the focus on what the law allows them to use.

Fair and careful instructions also matter because they reduce the chances of misinterpretation that could later lead to appeals or distrust in the system. If jurors misunderstand a part of the law, they might reach a verdict that does not reflect the true balance of proof. In such cases, a judge's clarification during the trial can prevent confusion and support a fair result. Judges also guide jurors on how to handle conflicting testimony, how to treat expert opinions, and how to consider physical or circumstantial evidence. The overall effect is to keep the process steady, predictable, and fair for everyone involved.

Ensuring Fairness in Trial Proceedings

Fairness in a trial means more than the outcome of one verdict. It means that the process itself treats all people with equal respect and gives everyone a real chance to present their side. A fair trial uses careful juror selection to minimize bias, clear courtroom rules to prevent unfair influence, and ongoing reminders to jurors about their duties and responsibilities.

Voir dire, the questions used to screen potential jurors, helps identify biases or conflicts that could affect impartiality. The judge and lawyers aim to keep a jury panel that can weigh the evidence without prejudice. Once a jury is seated, it is essential that all jurors have the opportunity to speak. The foreperson plays a crucial role in guiding discussions, but every juror's voice should be heard. Instructions about courtroom behavior—no talking outside the courtroom, no sharing case details, and treating others with respect—help maintain a calm, respectful environment where truth can emerge from careful discussion.

Outside factors can threaten fairness. Media coverage, for example, might shape people's perceptions before they hear all the facts. In some cases, judges may admonish the public, limit media access, or even sequester jurors to reduce outside influence. The courtroom also guards against unfair influence by allowing both sides to present evidence and cross-examine witnesses, ensuring that all relevant questions are explored and tested.

Two practical examples illustrate how fairness is pursued in real life. Example 1: A juror brings a personal assumption about a suspect's character into deliberations. The judge's instructions remind everyone to focus on evidence about the crime, not on stereotypes. The lawyers may also introduce clarifying questions during closing arguments to reset the focus. Example 2: A witness offers expert testimony that could be confusing. The judge allows the expert to explain in plain terms and invites the attorneys to contest the explanations, helping the jury understand the evidence on its own terms.

Troubleshooting common problems and quick fixes

1) Problem: Some jurors rely on stereotypes rather than evidence. Fix: The judge clarifies the standard of proof and emphasizes that verdicts must be based on admitted evidence and reasonable inferences from that evidence.

2) Problem: Jurors are unsure about how to weigh circumstantial evidence. Fix: Provide clear guidance on how circumstantial evidence can be enough when it points consistently to a conclusion and matches other proven facts.

3) Problem: Outside information from media shapes opinions. Fix: Court may limit or manage access to outside information and remind jurors to rely strictly on trial evidence and instructions.

4) Problem: A few jurors dominate the discussion. Fix: The foreperson and the judge ensure every juror has time to speak; the judge may guide the group to consider quieter perspectives.

5) Problem: The jury cannot reach a verdict. Fix: The judge may encourage continued deliberations or, in some cases, declare a mistrial if a verdict remains unattainable after extensive discussion.

Tools and resources

1) Plain-language summaries of jury instructions for jurors, written in simple terms to reinforce understanding during deliberations.

2) Mock trial templates and practice sheets that help students imagine how evidence is weighed and how reasonable doubt is evaluated.

3) Evidence evaluation checklists to help readers track how each piece of evidence supports or undermines guilt or innocence.

4) Courtroom behavior guidelines and quick-reference notes that remind readers of fair conduct, respect, and focus during trials.

In the next chapter: Preventing Wrongful Convictions and Ensuring Justice

1) Improving legal procedures and evidence standards,

2) The role of forensic science and expert testimony,

3) Community efforts to reduce wrongful accusations

Chapter 14

You will understand how to reduce wrongful convictions by improving procedures, using solid science, and building strong community awareness.

1) Improving legal procedures and evidence standards

You begin by thinking about how a fair decision happens. Good procedures mean questions are answered openly, and no part of the process is hurried or secret. In practice, that looks like clear rules about how evidence is collected, stored, and shared. It means everyone—defendants, lawyers, and judges—has access to the same information, and no key facts are kept hidden. It also means there are dependable checks to prevent mistakes from slipping through.

One big piece is how evidence is handled. Imagine a piece of physical evidence, like a shoeprint or a fiber sample. If the evidence isn't labeled and stored with a secure chain of custody, its usefulness can disappear in a courtroom. A well-run system keeps a careful record of who touched the item, when, and how it was analyzed. This helps prevent miscommunication and ensures the lab work can be trusted.

Another important part is the disclosure of exculpatory information—the facts that might favor the defendant. If a piece of evidence could undermine the prosecution's case or support the defendant's innocence, it should be shared promptly. Delays or omissions can tilt a verdict toward guilt even when innocence is possible.

Professional standards matter, too. Experts who testify should be qualified, use methods that have been tested and validated, and explain their limits. The goal is not to overwhelm a jury with technical jargon, but to make sure the science behind conclusions is sound and not overstated. Judges may require that an expert's conclusions be backed by reliable data and that any uncertainty is acknowledged.

In everyday terms, you want trial procedures that are transparent, consistent, and accountable. You want clear timelines for turning over evidence, standardized training for those handling evidence, and independent reviews when something looks off. When these safeguards are in place, the risk of a wrongful conviction drops.

To bring these ideas to life, consider two micro-scenarios. In the first, a lab technician uses a method that isn't widely accepted for the type of sample involved, and the result is treated as solid proof. A careful system would flag that method as questionable, require an alternative test, or demand peer-reviewed support before the result becomes part of the record. In the second scenario, a prosecutor with a strong case withholds a single exculpatory report. Even though the case might be winnable without it, the lack of disclosure creates a real danger that someone could be found guilty when they might be innocent. In both cases, fair procedures catch problems before verdicts are made.

What can you do as a reader or a future professional? Encourage clear checklists for evidence handling, insist on timely disclosure of all relevant information, and support education about how to interpret scientific results. Advocate for independent reviews of disputed evidence and for court rules that require validation of new forensic methods before they are admitted as proof. The goal is a system that minimizes mistakes and respects the rights of every person involved.

2) The role of forensic science and expert testimony

Forensic science can be a powerful ally for justice, but only when it is used carefully and honestly. You learn that not all methods are equally reliable in every situation, and every claim about evidence should come with a clear explanation of its limits. Experts should speak in ways that are understandable to non-specialists, and they should acknowledge what they do not know as part of their testimony. That honesty helps judges and juries weigh the facts more accurately.

DNA testing is a cornerstone of modern forensics. It can link a suspect to a crime scene with high accuracy when collected and analyzed correctly. But even DNA has limitations: contamination risks, partial results, or mixed samples can complicate conclusions. A careful expert will describe what the result means and what it does not prove, along with any potential uncertainties.

Fingerprints, tool marks, fibers, and other types of evidence also require careful handling and qualified interpretation. Some older techniques have been shown to be less reliable than once thought, so they must be evaluated against current standards and, if possible, supported by objective data. Experts should avoid presenting results as absolute truths when there is room for doubt, and they should be prepared to explain alternative explanations.

Cross-examination is a tool for testing strength and reliability. A skilled attorney will ask hard questions that reveal whether an expert's confidence matches the data, whether the analyst used a fair sample, or whether conclusions go beyond what the evidence can support. When experts are challenged in court, the risk of overreaching conclusions decreases, and the verdict becomes more grounded in solid reasoning.

Two micro-scenarios illustrate these ideas. First, imagine an expert testifying that a blood-spatter pattern proves how a crime happened. A rigorous approach would require the expert to show the underlying data, explain alternative interpretations, and acknowledge the limits of what the pattern can reveal. If those steps aren't taken, a jury might be swayed by a confident narrative rather than by careful analysis. In the second scenario, a lab report includes a statistical likelihood but does not explain what that probability means in practical terms. A careful defense attorney would press for plain-language explanations and for comparisons to known error rates, ensuring the jury understands how strong the evidence truly is.

You can nurture better use of forensic science by supporting policies that require validated methods, peer-reviewed research, and full transparency in reporting. Favor situations where experts provide clear, grounded explanations rather than sensational statements. When forensic testimony meets these standards, it strengthens justice rather than masking uncertainty behind technical language.

3) Community efforts to reduce wrongful accusations

Beyond courts and labs, communities play a vital role in preventing wrongful accusations. Reducing bias, improving education, and promoting fair treatment for all people helps create a safer, more just society. You can picture this as a collective effort that begins with everyday interactions and grows to larger institutions.

Education is a cornerstone. Teaching people—young and old—about how biases can influence decisions helps reduce snap judgments. This includes recognizing that assumptions about race, class, or background can cloud judgment and lead to unfair accusations. Schools, community centers, and media organizations all have a part to play by presenting information honestly and avoiding sensationalism that can fuel fear or prejudice.

Media coverage also matters. News reporting that sticks to verified facts, uses careful language, and presents multiple sides of a story helps the public understand what is known, what isn't, and why certain conclusions are tentative. Responsible reporting can prevent the spread of rumors that might lead to pressure on investigators or prosecutors to rush to a guilty verdict.

Community organizations provide support for people who face accusations. Legal aid clinics, counseling services, and volunteer mentors can help individuals understand their rights, navigate complex processes, and rebuild their lives if acquitted. Community oversight groups can review practices in police departments, courts, and laboratories to spot unfair patterns and push for improvements.

Restorative practices offer another approach. When appropriate, communities can explore ways to repair harm without automatically re-litigating every case. Restorative conversations, fair reintegration programs, and transparent reporting about errors can reduce stigma and help people move forward after a not guilty verdict.

Two micro-scenarios show the power of community action. In one, a local youth program teaches students about rights and responsibilities and includes role-play on reporting bias or harassment. The program helps young people recognize when an accusation might be influenced by prejudice and encourages them to seek fair, lawful resolutions. In another scenario, a neighborhood watch group partners with a legal clinic to ensure residents understand how to document concerns and access help if someone feels wrongfully accused. These efforts create a network that supports fairness and accountability across the community.

As you think about these three points, you can see how strengthening procedures, improving the science behind evidence, and building responsible communities work together. Each piece reduces the chance that a person is wrongly blamed for a crime and helps ensure that real guilt, when it exists, is proven in a careful, credible way.

In the next chapter, you will explore the Resources and Support for Those Cleared of Charges—learning about organizations offering legal aid and counseling, steps to restore reputation after acquittal, and moving forward after a not guilty verdict. In practical terms, you will discover where to turn for help, how to begin rebuilding your life after acquittal, and how communities can stand with you as you move forward.

Chapter 15

By the end of this chapter, you will know where to find legal aid and counseling, how to begin rebuilding your reputation after acquittal, and how to move forward with practical steps and support.

Organizations offering legal aid and counseling

1) Know the kinds of help you can get. You can usually access free or low-cost legal advice through nonprofit legal aid organizations, university or law-school clinics, and public defender systems. Many communities also offer victim-witness programs, which help with court-related stress and understanding next steps. Counseling services—whether for mental health, personal resilience, or family support—often partner with legal aid groups, so you can pursue legal and emotional support at the same time. You do not have to navigate this alone; organizations exist to guide you through the process in clear, respectful ways.

2) Check eligibility and scope. Legal aid is typically designed for people who meet income or special-status guidelines, but many clinics offer free initial consultations or sliding-scale fees. Schools and community centers may have student-friendly programs with simplified intake forms. Counselors and support services usually tailor their help to your age, situation, and goals. If you're unsure whether you qualify, ask the intake staff directly what options fit your circumstances. When you know what's available, you can choose the path that fits your needs without paying more than you can.

3) Reach out and ask what to expect. Start with a simple call, email, or in-person visit to the most appropriate organization. Prepare a brief description of your situation, what you hope to achieve, and any documents you have from the acquittal. Ask about intake steps, what to bring (such as your verdict documents or school records), confidentiality, and what the first meeting will cover. If transport or scheduling is a challenge, ask if they offer evenings, weekends, or virtual options. You deserve a clear path forward, not a long maze of questions.

4) Coordinate with other supports. Legal advice often pairs well with counseling, school or workplace support, and community resources. For example, a counselor can help you process emotions while a lawyer explains your rights and options. If you have a team of people helping you, keep a simple contact list and share updates you're comfortable sharing. This coordination reduces confusion and helps you move forward with confidence.

Examples and micro-scenarios

- Lina, 14, feels overwhelmed after her acquittal. Her school counselor connects her with a local legal aid clinic that offers free advice for students. Lina learns what documents to gather and what questions to ask, and she attends a no-cost intake session that clarifies her next steps. The process feels manageable because a trusted adult helps her navigate it.

- Kai, 16, wants to understand his options and protect his privacy. He contacts a national youth advocacy organization that provides a helpline and online resources. A staff member explains eligibility, outlines a plan to obtain legal aid, and helps him prepare for the first meeting without fear of judgment.

Steps you can take now

- Make a short list of nearby legal aid options and counseling services. Include at least three possibilities and note their contact methods and hours.

- Gather basic documents to bring to an intake: verdict paper, any court notices, and a record of any communication you've had about the case.

- Prepare a simple, honest summary of what you want to achieve—clarity about your rights, help with records, or guidance on rebuilding trust.

- Choose one main point of contact to start with, and set a concrete appointment within the next week if possible.

Steps to restore reputation after acquittal

1) Gather official documents and record what happened. Start by obtaining a certified copy of the acquittal verdict and any related court documents. These records are important for explaining your status to schools, employers, or future mentors. Keep copies in a secure place and note dates for when you might need them for records requests or expungement discussions.

2) Learn about record-clearing options. Depending on your jurisdiction, some charges can be sealed or expunged after acquittal, which may help with school admissions, job applications, and housing. Talk with your lawyer or a legal-aid counselor about what's possible in your area and what steps you'd need to take. Understand that rules vary—some places require wait times, while others have automatic processes for certain outcomes.

3) Communicate thoughtfully with schools and employers. When you need to share information, stick to the facts you are comfortable disclosing. A brief, calm explanation that you were acquitted and that you are moving forward can reduce speculation. If you're in school, ask a trusted counselor to help you craft a short message for administrators or teachers. If you work, a concise note to HR or a supervisor can help set the record straight.

4) Demonstrate consistent, positive behavior. Actions often speak louder than words. Attend classes or work regularly, complete assignments or duties on time, and participate in activities that reflect your true character. Build a track record you're proud of, and ask for references from teachers, mentors, or supervisors who can attest to your conduct and commitment.

Examples and micro-scenarios

- Ari, 15, is worried about his college prospects after acquittal. He obtains a sealed-record letter from the court and presents a brief, factual summary to his guidance counselor, who helps him prepare a clean, transparent explanation for his senior-year applications. Ari also joins a volunteer program to show his commitment to helping others.

- Maya, 17, wants to restore her reputation at a part-time job. She asks her supervisor for a quick meeting, brings a copy of the acquittal documents, and shares her plan to move forward—focusing on reliable attendance, open communication, and steady performance. Her straightforward approach reduces rumor spread and builds trust over time.

Moving forward after a not guilty verdict

1) Prioritize mental health and ongoing support. A not guilty verdict can still carry stress, stigma, or confusion. Seek counseling, peer support groups, or trusted mentors to process the experience. Establish a routine that includes sleep, healthy meals, physical activity, and time for reflection. Regular support helps you stay grounded as you rebuild your life.

2) Plan practical steps for daily life. Set realistic goals for school, work, and social life. Create a simple schedule that reduces reminders of the past while keeping you focused on the present. A small, achievable plan—like attending three study sessions per week or volunteering a few hours—can restore confidence and momentum.

3) Re-engage with community and mentors. Rebuild connections through clubs, teams, or volunteer activities where you can meet supportive people who see your strengths. Seek mentors who can offer guidance, practical advice, and encouragement as you move forward. Positive, steady relationships create a foundation for your ongoing growth.

4) Consider civil actions only with guidance. If you believe you suffered lasting harm from the process, talk with a trusted advisor about your options. Civil actions, when appropriate, require careful legal consideration and clear aims. Don't rush; gather facts, advice, and realistic expectations before making any decisions.

Examples and micro-scenarios

- Omar, 16, feels judged at school after his acquittal. He joins a community-service club and begins tutoring younger students. Within weeks, teachers notice improved focus and a more positive attitude, and classmates start inviting him to participate in group projects again.

- Jade, 15, considers whether to pursue a civil action after acquittal. She timelines the options with her counselor, gathers evidence of impact, and decides to proceed only after discussing risk and potential outcomes with a trusted attorney. Her cautious approach keeps her informed without creating unnecessary stress.

Troubleshooting: common problems and quick fixes

- Problem: You feel overwhelmed by conflicting advice from different organizations.

Fix: Pick one primary contact to guide you through the process, and ask them to help you coordinate with other services.

- Problem: You worry about privacy or what to disclose publicly.

Fix: Ask about confidentiality and what information is essential to share. Keep records of who has access to your information.

- Problem: Speak or act before you understand the rules about record clearing.

Fix: Get a clear explanation from a legal advisor about eligibility, timelines, and steps. Don't rush to share personal details before you know what's safe to disclose.

- Problem: You don't hear back after contacting resources.

Fix: Follow up with a brief, polite message or call. If delays persist, ask about alternative contacts or walk-in hours.

Tools and templates

- Intake contact script: "Hello, I'm seeking guidance after a not guilty verdict. I'd like to understand what legal aid options are available, the eligibility requirements, and the first steps I should take."

- Simple email to request assistance: "Subject: Request for legal aid and counseling. Dear [Organization], I recently received an acquittal and I'd like to learn about free or low-cost options for legal advice and emotional support. Please tell me what I should prepare for intake and how soon I can meet with a counselor or attorney."

- One-page plan for moving forward after acquittal: a short outline that lists documents, contacts, goals, and a weekly schedule.

Conclusion and transition

You have practical steps to access help, to repair your public image, and to chart a clear path forward after a not guilty verdict. The next chapter will explore how the legal system treats not guilty outcomes in more detail, including the rights you retain and the safeguards that protect you as you continue your journey. Thank you for reading this chapter and for your courage in seeking support. Thank you, reader, for staying with the book as you move forward.

www.ingramcontent.com/pod-product-compliance
Lightning Source LLC
LaVergne TN
LVHW082358200926
848481LV00012B/3605